How They
MADE IT

D1332816

How They
MADE IT

Inspirational stories of how others
succeeded in their dream
job and how you can too

Edited by Lucy Smith and Jessica Spencer

How They Made It. Inspirational stories of how others succeeded in their dream job and how you can too

This first edition published in 2012 by Trotman Publishing, an imprint of Crimson Publishing Ltd Westminster House, Kew Road, Richmond, Surrey TW9 2ND

British Library Cataloguing in Publication Data
A catalogue record for this book is available from the British Library

ISBN 978 1 84455 461 4

Typeset by IDSUK (DataConnection) Ltd
Printed and bound in the UK by Ashford Colour Press, Gosport, Hants

Contents

Acknowledgements   vii

Introduction   viii

Architect
Ruth Reed   1

Athlete
Chris Tomlinson   11

Chef and restaurateur
Paul Ainsworth   21

Children's poet and author
Michael Rosen   33

Classical musician
Joshua Bell   45

Composer
Eric Whitacre   55

Creative director
Paul Brazier   67

Critic
Mark Kermode   75

DJ
Andi Durrant   85

Fashion magazine editor-in-chief
Trish Halpin   97

Food creative
Rachel Khoo 105

Genre writer
Barbara Machin 117

Ichthyologist
Dr Eugenie Clarke 125

Musician
Johnny Marr 137

News broadcaster
Krishnan Guru-Murthy 147

Photographer
Steve Bloom 157

Pilot
Dave Barrett 165

Product designer
Emma Bridgewater 175

Screenwriter
Paul Abbott 187

Soprano
Laura Wright 197

TV producer
Tim Hincks 205

Winemaker
Sam Lindo 213

Chapter authors 223

Acknowledgements

Our thanks go to all the people who gave their time to kindly share their stories for the book, giving frank and insightful accounts into their career journeys and providing really useful advice for our readers.

We also thank our graduate writers, who have worked tirelessly on this project, securing people to feature in the book, conducting interviews and writing quality chapters, often in addition to full-time work.

Finally, we would like to thank everyone at Crimson Publishing for the time and effort they have put into collating and producing the book.

Introduction

In the current climate, it's harder than ever for graduates and people looking to change their career to secure that ultimate dream job. With the Office for National Statistics citing one in five graduates as unemployed, as well as one in three graduates employed in a low-skilled job in 2012, the future isn't looking particularly promising. While this may make you feel despondent, securing a place on a graduate scheme and climbing your way to the top is not the only route to success. Sometimes, you need to take matters into your own hands.

We decided to compile this book to look at how some of the most successful people in their fields made it to the top and, crucially, to ask their advice for other people hoping to do the same. We have tracked their stories from the very beginning, asking about what spurred them on, their career highs and lows and what their work actually involves on a day-to-day basis. What we've achieved, we hope, is a collection of real-life stories that are not only interesting but also inspiring.

Why have we chosen these people?

There are lots of successful people out there in a range of glamorous and exciting careers so how did we decide who to feature? Well, we wanted to make sure we focused on individuals who have both an entertaining and inspiring career story to tell. We also wanted to cover people from different ages and backgrounds working in a variety of industries, highlighting many different paths to success, from troubled beginnings to fate-filled destinies. This is primarily a careers book and as such we hope you will find plenty of advice and guidance for success in these stories, from following a traditional path to being completely unconventional, so even if your dream job isn't covered we hope you can still take away the principles of what it takes to succeed.

Why graduate writers?

There are two reasons why we chose recent graduates to write the profiles for this book. Firstly, because they (you) are our target audience, so in this sense we were able to ensure the profiles would actually be useful and relevant to our readers. And secondly, we wanted to give creative and bright individuals the chance to be living examples of what we want the book to show.

The message that shines through in so many of the stories is the need for self-belief, determination and, above all, perseverance. When no one at the indie record label Rough Trade would listen to The Smiths, Johnny Marr stood outside in the loading bay for hours on end until he found someone to give their CD to, and when Tim Hincks was determined to work in television and had no useful contacts he took to writing to everyone with a 'posh' sounding name in the *Radio Times*. These stories show that sometimes an unconventional and creative approach is what is needed to reach your goal.

So what is the difference between people who nearly make it and those who actually do? Unstoppable, unrelenting drive and ambition – there's no magic secret other than that. Despite reaching huge levels of success, these are ordinary people who worked hard to get to where they are today. Moreover, they took risks to fulfil their passions, like Rachel Khoo who gave up a stable, well-paid job in the city to live and cook in a studio apartment in Paris. More often than not, the people featured in this book have gone against the 'typical graduate route', taking chances and knocking on doors in search of opportunities. They followed their dreams, and hopefully, after reading this book, you'll feel inspired to do the same.

More than anything, we hope you enjoy reading the stories as much as we enjoyed writing them, and who knows, in a few years' time our next edition could be featuring you!

ARCHITECT

Ruth Reed

Current title: Director of Professional Studies, PGDip Architectural Practice, Birmingham City University

Age and DOB: 55 (b. 1956)

First job: architectural assistant to national house builder Whelmar Ltd

Other careers: founder of Reed Architects, consultant planning inspector, part-time partner of Green Planning Solutions

Most well known for: first female RIBA president 2009-2011

Her career advisor may have felt that architecture was for men, but Ruth Reed had discovered 'something very special' about the subject and she was not about to let a small thing like being a woman get in her way. Since defiantly choosing to study architecture at Sheffield University, Ruth has proven her worth time and time again, even becoming the first female president of the Royal Institute of British Architects (RIBA) in 2009. In between this, the focused architect has juggled motherhood, setting up her own practice and becoming a planning inspector, before turning her hand to university teaching. Alongside her success, Ruth has dealt with her fair share of business blows, and in 2001, foot and mouth disease threatened to destroy her practice. However, she has learnt a valuable lesson in versatility along the way and has 'managed to turn compromises into advantages'.

Architectural epiphany

Growing up in Shrewsbury on the Welsh border, the only girl among three brothers, Ruth has always been familiar with masculine environments. Despite neither of her parents attending university, there was 'a general assumption' among her family that Ruth, the diligent student and head prefect, would attend. In her mid-teens, Ruth visited the iconic site of King's College Chapel in Cambridge and describes the experience as 'a sort of epiphany': 'just as music gets you going, I realised that buildings had even more of an effect on me', she says. Ruth became immediately determined to be an architect and with the help of an 'inspirational' art teacher at the state grammar school she attended from 1968 to 1975, she developed the creativity and imagination required for the task. However, while her family did not doubt the grade A student's potential, her careers master quickly warned her not to follow her passion, as the architecture course at university was too long and he assumed she would want to get married and have children by the end of it.

Undeterred by the careers master's doubts, Ruth describes his unwelcomed advice as 'probably the best thing anybody could have said to me because of course I was instantly determined to prove him wrong'. Ruth went straight to Sheffield University from the sixth form at the age of 18 and knew instantly that she had made the right decision: 'I couldn't get over that I was actually doing what I wanted to do *all* of the time.' At school, Ruth was inevitably forced to study some subjects that did not interest her, but at Sheffield she discovered that she was fascinated by all aspects of architecture. She had truly found her passion.

Making compromises

After finishing her undergraduate studies in 1978, the passionate student went on to achieve her diploma in architecture in 1981, followed by a master's degree in landscape in 1982. In the meantime, Ruth was offered her first experience of employment, working as an architectural assistant to a national house builder in South Yorkshire in 1981, for a company named Whelmar Ltd. This job was far from her dream occupation, as it was only loosely related to her degree and did not allow for her to be involved with the actual building of housing estates. However, entering the job market at the beginning of a recession in the North of England, Ruth learnt her first lesson in compromise and quickly accepted the offer. Despite her reservations, by showing a little versatility, Ruth laid the foundations of many of her future career successes.

While working with Whelmar Ltd, Ruth designed the plan of a set of sheltered housing properties and although she would have preferred to design the actual buildings, this gave her valuable experience in site layout. Moreover, Ruth also discovered her interest in landscape design and developed her knowledge of the governmental regulations to which architects must adhere. These early experiences would serve to make Ruth more marketable in the future: 'I've learnt that everything is an opportunity, even though it may feel like a compromise, you'd be surprised what you can make of it later on.' Ruth remained in her first job until 1983. From then on, she continued to further her experience and managed to get back on track to the work that had originally interested her, working as an architect for commercial projects with Hadfield Cawkwell Davidson in Sheffield until 1987.

By showing a little versatility, Ruth laid the foundations of many of her future career successes.

In the same year, Ruth gave birth to her first child and so decided to work part time at South Yorkshire Housing Association. Working for the largest supplier of care and supported housing in the region, Ruth was involved with designing many such properties. She remained in this role for two years, beginning as an architect and quickly moving on to senior architect. Ruth describes the housing association as a 'good employer', as they understood her need to juggle raising her daughter with her work. However, after leaving the housing association in 1990 to move with her family to mid-Wales, Ruth gave birth to her second daughter in 1991 and discovered that not all employers were as willing to be 'saddled with maternity pay and part-time working'. Ruth remembers: 'I was aware then that there were issues about being a woman.' However, this was the only time that Ruth felt the presence of such issues and despite at times feeling that it was 'a bit spooky', walking into an all-male building site, this never discouraged her. After facing issues of employment during pregnancy, undeterred as ever Ruth 'simply changed track and went self-employed'.

Going it alone

While Ruth may have been encouraged to become self-employed for the sake of her children, this in itself was a brave business venture, which involved starting up her own small, rural practice – Reed Architects – in mid-Wales, working mostly with customers who were self-building properties. Having put in place a formula that allowed her to work and raise her children from home, Ruth found this phase of her career 'thoroughly enjoyable' and says that 'both children looking back say that they had lovely, happy childhoods'. However, while her family life was thriving, Ruth admits that she had a great loss of confidence in her career at this time: 'I felt like I'd vanished because my identity had always been as an architect, not as a mother and housewife.' Struggling with small domestic jobs at little profit, Ruth began to wonder whether she would ever again become a 'proper architect', making real money on larger domestic or commercial projects. To make matters worse, in 2001, foot and mouth disease struck the UK and rural mid-Wales 'essentially shut down for a year and a half'. Ruth watched her turnover drop to a third of what it had been and she entered into a 'mini recession'. Yet again though, Ruth overcame what could have been a disaster by showing flexibility in the face of adversity and she began looking for work as a consultant planning inspector.

Ironically, by the time Ruth had landed a job in 2002, business was picking up again in mid-Wales, and Ruth relied on assistance from her then husband to run the practice. As a planning inspector she mostly dealt with appeals made by people who had been rejected planning permission. Ruth's time as a planning inspector helped her to understand the number of errors that are often made in issuing planning permission, which assisted her work within her own practice. Yet, despite being an insightful occupation,

Ruth found planning inspecting a lonely career, as much of her time was spent working on writing representation cases for those who wished to appeal against planning permission rejections. Consequently, Ruth left the role in 2004 and concentrated solely on her practice.

Despite the hurdles along the way, Ruth managed Reed Architects for 13 years, by the end of which she had turned over 'a reasonable profit' and earned the practice a reputation for gaining planning approval within areas of the tightest rural planning constraints.

Discovering new skills

In the early years of running her own practice, Ruth became involved with the Royal Society of Architects in Wales (RSAW). As part of RIBA, the RSAW works to achieve and maintain better architectural standards in Wales. Feeling isolated as a self-employed mother in the countryside of mid-Wales, Ruth decided to join 'for as much social as professional development'. She explains, 'I used the RSAW really as a prop to get me out, talking to like-minded people.' Ruth was instantly popular with the society, with whom she discussed the quality of architectural practice in Wales and she was soon approached to run for president. However, the dedicated mum of two refused the offer many times while her daughters were still small: 'I think there is a time for everything and women have the opportunity to do a lot of different things in their lives. You've just got to recognise that you can't do it all at once, because you'll kill yourself.' Consequently, Ruth waited until 2003 to apply for the two-year presidency and she held the position until 2005.

Ruth simultaneously involved herself with RIBA, where she gained experience as a professional examiner of training architects. Similarly, she had previously gained some teaching experience as a visiting tutor at the Welsh School of Architecture from 1993. In 2006, Ruth decided to leave mid-Wales for personal reasons and put her teaching practice into full-time use, becoming Director of the Postgraduate Diploma in Architectural Practice at the Birmingham School of Architecture. Leaving Reed Architects to the care of her former husband, Ruth moved to Birmingham, where her first job was to completely re-draft and re-evaluate the course.

Ruth addressing a meeting at the Worshipful Company of Architects. The company supports architectural education and scholarship.

'I think there is a time for everything and women have the opportunity to do a lot of different things in their lives. You've just got to recognise that you can't do it all at once, because you'll kill yourself.'

First female president

Meanwhile, Ruth was becoming increasingly involved with RIBA and despite joining the RSAW originally for social purposes, she soon learned that she had impressive leadership skills. In 2005 Ruth was elected by the Regional Councils as vice president of RIBA. Discovering she had more time since moving to Birmingham and giving up the practice, Ruth decided in 2009 to run for presidency of the RIBA. It was then that Ruth truly understood the value of the early compromises she had made in her career decisions, as the fact that she had been a planning inspector and had worked for a national house builder made her stand out as a candidate. In 2009, Ruth was elected for a two-year term as the first female president of RIBA, which works with government to improve the design quality of public buildings, new homes and new communities, as well as working with universities to improve the quality of degrees in architecture. As president, Ruth was able to use her experience at Birmingham to evaluate the ways in which architectural studies should be adapted so that students are made aware of how to transfer their university learning into actual architectural practice.

Entering as president in 2009 during a global financial crisis, Ruth also had to discuss measures of making the best use of scarce financial resources. She campaigned hard with government to ensure that the recession did not lead to a drop in architectural standards. Ruth's task was made particularly challenging with the upheaval in Westminster and the

Ruth was elected as the president of RIBA in 2009 and served in the position for two years.

arrival of the coalition government in 2010. Under new government, huge changes were made to the architectural planning process, and as president, Ruth oversaw them all, evidence of which can be seen in the new National Planning Policy Framework. Despite the 'media hoo-ha' surrounding the first female president of the RIBA, Ruth 'just got on with it', remaining characteristically unfazed by her minority position as a woman. Speaking in 2009, she said, 'I hope that by example I will encourage more women to remain in architecture.'

During her presidency, Ruth had to split her time between London and Birmingham, while also travelling to other regions to discuss architectural policy. Ruth's endless schedule took both physical and emotional endurance and on reflection she struggles to understand how she coped: 'I have to look at my diary to believe I can fit it all in.' Ruth's passion for architecture alone inspired her to take on such a demanding responsibility, as the role of president of RIBA is unpaid. Despite the strain that it put on her timetable, Ruth maintains that the opportunity to travel and meet people and even to have influence at Westminster was 'the most extraordinary and satisfying of experiences'.

Despite the 'media hoo-ha' surrounding the first female president of the RIBA, Ruth 'just got on with it', remaining characteristically unfazed by her minority position as a woman.

Exploring other options

Since the end of her two-year presidency, Ruth's schedule has been lighter, but she is nonetheless as driven as ever. Remaining actively involved with RIBA, chairing the planning group and acting as immediate past president, Ruth continues to travel down to London around once a week to fulfil these duties. Moreover, since 2007 Ruth has been a minor partner in her brother's planning consultancy, Green Planning Solutions, which focuses on obtaining planning permission in developmentally constrained areas. While the role does not require her to visit the practice often, Ruth believes that being a partner in a firm assists her teaching, as it keeps her informed of the pressures with which the architecture industry is faced.

Ruth's ambitious nature appears to have been inherited by both of her daughters, as one is studying medicine, while the other is completing her PhD in computer science. Ruth hopes she has taught them that 'it is perfectly possible to do whatever you want to do and to enjoy what you're doing'. For Ruth, enjoying her career is the most important requirement. She modestly admits that architecture has never made her rich and she has never reached the 'dizzy heights of running a big London practice'. However, she explains, 'what I have done is enjoyed my engagement with architecture and enjoyed talking about it with the rest of the world.' Through careful planning in difficult times and always having another option at the ready, Ruth has discovered that sometimes plan B is the more favourable option. Consequently, the architect has built herself into a unique and marketable business woman, which she insists is a great asset in a crowded market. Currently, Ruth is under extreme pressure to return to her practice and although she has no plans to leave her position at Birmingham, she is no stranger to splitting her time between responsibilities. Ruth is yet to make a decision on this, but she asserts that 'anything is possible'.

ATHLETE

Chris Tomlinson

Current title: professional long jumper

Age and DOB: 30 (b. 1981)

First job: helping with his brother's clothes shop

Other careers: personal trainer and property developer

Most well known for: British record holder for long jump

Since breaking a seemingly undefeatable British long jump record at the age of 20, British athlete Chris Tomlinson has continued to beat his personal best time and time again over the last 10 years while collecting a host of medals along the way. However it has been no walk in the park for the Middlesbrough-born long jumper, as he has dealt with a series of devastatingly timed injuries that have led to some disappointing competition results. After failing to progress through to the final of the Beijing Olympics, Chris was forced to consider sideline careers. Yet the easy-going northerner has not been deterred by his misfortune, accepting that the potential for injury 'is all part and parcel of what I've chosen to do in life'.

The sky's the limit

Born and raised in Middlesbrough, Chris had his first experience of athletics through sprinting for Mandale Harriers Athletics Club at the age of 11. His sister had run for the county briefly and his father had played tennis for Middlesbrough. Consequently, going to the local athletics track with his father one day after school 'seemed like natural progression'. Despite being the fastest in his class, Chris did not predict the reception that he would receive from the club and on the very first session, coach Brian Davison predicted that 'the sky's the limit for him'.

However, Chris believed that sprinting was not about to make him the record breaker he is today: 'I was fast but I certainly didn't have the potential to get to where I've got.' It wasn't until he took up the triple jump and long jump in his early teens that Chris discovered where his true talent lay and he went on to win a number of amateur athletics age group titles for both events from the age of 15. Despite training six to eight hours a week, the young athlete continued to study and after leaving Nunthorpe Secondary School he went on to complete his A levels at sixth form college. For Chris, the decision to remain committed to his athletics throughout his school career was an easy one: 'I wasn't thick but I certainly wasn't the smartest kid in the class. I was probably never going to study astrophysics and chemistry at Oxford or anything.' His school career may not have been record breaking, but with a bit of maturity and a lot more practice, his long jumping would be.

From recreation to record breaking

As an 18-year-old college student, Chris was given the opportunity to represent Great Britain in the World Junior Long Jumping Championships. Acknowledging that he had not yet reached this competitive level in the triple jump, Chris moved away from this event for a while to focus on his long jump, with the intention of returning to the triple jump after the competition. However, when Chris eventually began practising the triple jump again, he discovered that his body was no longer strong enough for it and so he drifted away from the discipline. Meanwhile, his long jump was going from strength to strength and he made it through to the final of the World Junior Championships. Unfortunately Chris 'messed up' in the competition and finished in 12th which was a big disappointment. Consequently, he feels that finishing college and concentrating exclusively on his athletics was a major turning point in his career. 'When I look back now, that was the big difference. I left college and ate, slept and breathed athletics. I was like a sponge, soaking up as much experience as possible.'

The record success led to Chris being offered lottery funding from the government, thus becoming a 'tax-paying professional long jumper'.

This level of commitment came at a price and Chris remembers watching his friends getting jobs, enjoying nice cars and socialising, while he relied on financial support from his parents and a part-time job at his brother's clothes shop to support his passion. Chris admits that sacrificing everything to his sport was a huge gamble, but not one he would ever change. Thanks to his decision to stay on at school until the age of 18, Chris would always have the opportunity to attend university at a later date; however his career in athletics could not be postponed any further. Without his intense level of commitment in these crucial years, Chris believes he would have gone off to university, got distracted and given up on his dreams by his mid-twenties – a thought which is incomprehensible to the multi-Olympian today: 'I wouldn't necessarily advise anyone to do what I did, but at the time it seemed to be more a decision from the heart than the head.'

In Chris's case, his heart was proved right and on 13 April 2002, he jumped 8.27m at Tallahassee, Florida, beating Lynn Davies' British long jump record of 8.23m, which had previously remained unbroken for

34 years. Placing him among the world's top 10 long jumpers in 2002, this was the jump to kickstart Chris's career. Just 22 months after leaving college, Chris was quickly approached by a host of sponsors, before he eventually agreed to sign with Japanese kit company ASICS. Furthermore, the record success led to Chris being offered lottery funding from the government, thus becoming a 'tax-paying professional long jumper'.

Pushing through the pain

Things continued to look up for the young record breaker and in 2002 he won the European Cup and finished sixth in the Commonwealth Games. Moreover, not only had Chris smashed a seemingly frozen record, he had done so three months after breaking both his wrists in a freak weightlifting accident. Yet, unfortunately, this inopportunely timed injury was to set the precedent for the next few years of his career. Chris pushed himself to the limit in 2004, setting a national indoor record at the World Championships in Budapest, winning the European Cup for the second time and finishing fifth in the Athens Olympics. However, he received a heavy blow the following year, when he sustained enough injuries to miss most of the season. Experiencing such disappointment shortly after a string of successes, Chris struggled with the impact of his injuries. 'When you're doing well everyone wants a piece of you – when you're injured you're soon forgotten about and it's difficult.' Rather than accepting his need to rest, Chris continued to push himself, having moved to Newcastle to be closer to his coach, Peter Stanley, with whom he had trained since the age of 15. With hindsight Chris believes he should have taken a well-deserved break, but he had taken a huge gamble in his youth and he was beginning to wonder if it had been worth it. 'It felt like I'd sacrificed everything in my life to jump a long way and I hadn't necessarily gained as much as I'd sacrificed.'

Unfortunately, this was not to be the last of Chris' misfortunes and in 2008 he tore his calf muscle at the London Grand Prix at Crystal Palace, just three weeks before he was due to compete at the Olympic Games in Beijing. A mere five days before his jump, Chris received the much-anticipated scan results that allowed him to finally fly out to China. However, his injuries destroyed his hopes of a medal as he failed to reach the final. Chris experienced similar disappointment in 2011, when he sustained a knee injury three weeks before the World Championships in Daegu, South Korea. This time Chris qualified through to the finals, but finished in an unsatisfactory 11th place. Consequently, for Chris, 'injury is

Chris has enjoyed a number of successes for Great Britain throughout his long jump career.

the toughest thing to deal with, especially as it's not just a job, it's a passion and a dream'. However, with such 'rollercoaster' highs and lows in his career, Chris has gained the great psychological strength that is required to be an athlete and is now able to view his misfortunes as a learning curve. 'I've realised that you can't get so wrapped up in your athletics, it's not fair on the people around you. Every time you have a bad jump or every time you get slightly injured you could just mope around the house for weeks on end but you've got to pick your chin up.'

Learning to cope

Despite his injuries, Chris has had an impressive career in the 10 years since he first put his name in the record books. In June 2007, Chris broke his own British record, increasing his jump by a further 2cm. In the same year, Chris moved to London with his now-wife Lucia and appointed Frank Attoh as his new coach in 2008, with whom he remains today. After 13 years with Peter Stanley, Chris acknowledged that it was time to move on, however, he nonetheless felt some sadness at the thought of leaving his original coach.

As he matured, Chris' working relationship with Peter and then Frank developed into a friendship and Chris feels that having a good rapport with the coach is 'crucial' for an athlete. In the same year as appointing

Frank, Chris improved his indoor record by 1cm, before achieving an Indoor World Championships silver medal in Valencia. Since then Chris has had competition from fellow Brit Greg Rutherford, who defeated the outdoor record in 2009, only for Chris to reclaim the title in 2011, jumping an impressive 8.35m. Although Rutherford managed to match this jump the following year, Chris is far from disheartened by the competition: 'it spurs me on. Records are there to be broken.'

Despite his injuries, Chris has had an impressive career in the 10 years since he first put his name in the record books.

Chris believes that having two athletes at the top of their game can only be a good thing, giving Britain an even greater chance when competing against the top long jumpers in the world. He generously accepts 'if it has to be in my sport, it has to be in my sport'. However, Chris admits that he is not always as gracious in the face of opposition. 'When I'm training or competing, I'm a total knob head. I don't think about it, it's subconscious.' Chris describes his two different personalities, which he has for work and home and he believes that keeping perspective is how he copes with the battle between the highs and lows of his career. 'You can't take your frustrations out on other people. As soon as I do anything competitive you see a different side to me, but I like to think that off-track I'm quite a chilled out, relaxed bloke.'

A realistic approach

Chris's unpredictable occupation has also taught him to keep his career options open and he consequently maintains a sideline profession as a property developer. Faced with the reality that he will have to work after retirement from long jumping, Chris started buying houses and flats a few years ago and spends around an hour every morning dealing with the essential admin. He explains, 'if you're a footballer you live in a different world. It's not like that for athletes; it's a case of putting stuff in place for when I do retire.' While there are a variety of sources of income for athletes, from lottery grants which also fund private healthcare, to sponsorship from big brands, it has been important for Chris to maintain his reputation in order to ensure a good income: 'if you want to own a house and pay bills you kind of have to be in the top 10 in the world.' Unfortunately Chris' sponsor, ASICS, dropped him in 2007, but thanks to continued support from lottery funding, he managed to continue to subsidise his training. The prize money from competitions is another big source of income for Chris and having under-performed at the Beijing Olympics, the sensible athlete trained for his coaching badges in 2008 and also became a fully qualified personal trainer. However, Chris did very little work as a coach or personal trainer before his success in athletics picked up again and as a competitor in the 2012 London Olympics, he is now sponsored by a variety of brands, including Adidas, Liberty Insurance, Alfa Romeo and Mitchum deodorant. Yet Chris, sensibly, has laid the foundations for a career in coaching and personal training, should he need to return to it in the future.

In 2008 the multi-Olympian married actress and former Miss Newcastle Lucia Rovardi, and settling down further influenced his decision to consider other career paths. Having met at sixth form college, aged 17, the couple have learnt to be flexible around each other's work commitments over the last 13 years and Lucia is extremely supportive of her husband's career. On 15 March 2012, she gave birth to their first child, Raphael Rovardi Tomlinson and for the first few weeks relied on the support of family and friends while her husband was in Portugal, training with the Olympic team. Now back at home, Chris leads a busy schedule and after dealing with his property developing business every morning and heading to the track to train for two or three hours, he finds time to spend with his son, before heading out for the second round of his training in the evening. In the meantime Chris also has to attend regular physiotherapy sessions and he believes that he would never juggle it all without the help of his wife. 'We've been together a long time and she understands what it takes to be an athlete. She's great.'

Chris has laid the foundations for a career in coaching and personal training, should he need to return to it in the future.

More jumping ahead

During the build-up to the Olympics, even more of Chris' time was taken up with photo-shoots and campaigns. However, 'chilled out' Chris takes the commercial side of the Olympics in his stride: 'I know some athletes absolutely love it, but for me personally it's just something that has to be

As part of the London Olympics build-up, Chris took part in a number of high-profile photo-shoots and campaigns.

done.' Aged 30, the world indoor and European medallist takes his training very seriously, viewing all other aspects of his work as secondary. Yet, he insists he will not be forcing his son into athletics. 'I don't think I'm going to be a pushy father. If he was in the same position that I was in at 18, I don't know that I'd advise him to do what I did but we'll see. As long as he's doing something that he enjoys, that's the main thing for me.' Nevertheless, Chris believes that athletics is versatile enough to suit anyone.

Chris may have developed a sensible attitude to alternative careers since his disappointment at Beijing in 2008, but his faith in his athletic capability has not waned. He has slowly recovered from the surgery to his knee, to rectify the injury he incurred in July 2011 and has learnt from his past mistakes of over-stretching himself, deciding to miss out on the 2012 Indoor World Championships. Had Chris jumped his personal best of 8.35m in the 2008 Olympics, he would have taken home the gold and he remains confident that he has the potential to jump even further. Now that the Olympics are over (Chris finished 6th), Chris may just allow himself a few months of relaxation – his first real break since leaving school. Yet, he is adamant that he will not be retiring any time soon and even hopes to eventually compete in the triple jump once again. The multi-Olympian argues that while some people believe 30 to be old for an athlete, he is improving with age and experience: 'I'll just keep going and going until I stop enjoying it.'

'There is an event for everybody. If you're no good at sprinting, you can try shot-put or jumping. Once you've discovered what you enjoy, you just need to put your head down and work at it.'

CHEF AND RESTAURATEUR

Paul Ainsworth

Current title: chef and restaurateur

Age and DOB: 33 (b. 1979)

First job: paper round

Other careers: countless odd jobs

Most well known for: winning the dessert course on the *Great British Menu* in 2011 and his Padstow restaurants Paul Ainsworth at Number 6 and Rojano's in the Square

The paths our lives take often seem to be an inexpressible mixture of good fortune and hard work, but it is hard to believe how close Paul Ainsworth, a winner of *Great British Menu* and successful chef and restaurateur, came to not working within the food industry. Presented with four work experience options as a teenager, fate's roll of the dice landed on a hotel when it could so easily have pushed him into a sports shop, accountancy firm or roadside services. His natural flair in the kitchen has led to him working in some of the best restaurants in the UK, owning his own restaurant, expanding to open a second and winning one of the most prestigious competitions and awards in the industry.

The industry of youth

Paul's 'story isn't one of those where I sat at my grandmother's knee as a kid podding peas. I didn't have this love of food.' Born in 1979 in Southampton, Paul was introduced into the world of hospitality and hard work from an early age as his parents ran a guest-house, often working from 6am to very late at night. He was brought up in a strict household pervaded with a strong work ethic and an understanding of the value of money. Youth was not an excuse to be idle and in the search for new ways to fill his pockets and keep busy Paul took on countless jobs, both in the guest-house and out. By the age of 12 he had paper rounds, shifts in a newsagent, night shifts in a fruit and vegetable merchant and sold household items for a catalogue company – all on top of guest-house chores and schoolwork. A considerably industrious young man, Paul did not yet know he was going to be a chef; he enjoyed the experience of business and earning money drove his choices.

It was only work experience in a hotel and working under a hard task-master of a German chef that first attracted Paul to the kitchen. Little did he know that this chef would be the first in a long line of such employers, including the likes of Gary Rhodes, Gordon Ramsay and Marcus Wareing. It is obvious that the discipline of these chefs, as well as that of his parents, is something Paul is thankful for, something that he has valued and taken into all areas of his career. He is open about the importance of people who guide him and keep him on the straight and narrow, 'especially with my type of character'.

Learning by earning

When working in the kitchen turned into working for a local restaurant, it seemed that a career was mapping itself out and at the age of 16 he enrolled at Southampton City College, studying catering and hospitality. Though studying taught him the principles, Paul liked to learn by earning and was reluctant to give up the income of a job, so he worked as a waiter at The Star Hotel at the same time. Fearful of being thrown off the course, Paul did not tell anyone at college about his 'independent learning' at the university of life and not surprisingly his attendance suffered – especially since he would often work the breakfast shift before college.

When it became uncertain whether Paul would continue for a third year, his mix of talent, enthusiasm and hard work was rewarded – a legendary connection was made in the classroom. One of his tutors, Martin Nash, happened to be godfather to Gary Rhodes' children and Gary called the college looking for fresh talent to join his kitchen team at the London restaurant, Gary Rhodes in the Square. As an aspiring chef, Paul found it is hard to ignore the bright lights and food culture of London but high rent prices had kept the thought of it away from his mind. Only Gary's offer to cover Paul's hotel bill for the first three months, until he had saved enough to rent, made the move possible. So in 1998 with such a prestigious opportunity open to him Paul became one of Gary Rhodes' commis chefs. It is obvious that as a person, chef and businessman Gary would be a positive and formative influence, an essential catalyst in taking Paul's career to the next level.

A considerably industrious young man, Paul did not yet know he was going to be a chef; he enjoyed the experience of business and earning money drove his choices.

Bright lights and hot kitchens

In the heat of a professional kitchen, the pressure of constant performance and the collision of personalities and perfectionism bubbles like violently hot water. Much younger than most of the staff, at only 19, Paul found himself thrown into this intimidating environment but he seemed to find his feet, working with the philosophy that you have to 'give it your all, you only have one chance'. Despite the initial nerves of being a junior in a professional kitchen after a year, he stopped getting told off as much, stopped making mistakes, and thought 'yes, I can do this'. For any young chef, Paul discovered that it was his enthusiasm, dedication and willingness to spend time in the kitchen and learn that got him noticed: 'when you're a young chef, time in the kitchen is utterly invaluable'. He found that no matter how difficult it was, he loved it and it was his ability to cope within that environment that confirmed his future.

Gary Rhodes was the man who gave Paul his big break and who opened up the possibility for him to achieve something worthy of his potential. But after two years with Gary, Paul began looking for new opportunities to stretch his talent and enhance his experience in the kitchen. On his regular trips home to Southampton, Paul's coach passed the restaurant of

Paul worked in professional kitchens from a young age, refining his skills for the future.

a formidable chef who was to offer him exactly that. Gordon Ramsay has an even fiercer reputation in the industry than he does on television but he is just as respected, so when Paul bumped into him in the street, he couldn't resist asking for advice. Not satisfied with being told to 'keep doing what you're doing' Paul rang Gordon's restaurant that afternoon to see if there were any vacancies. He was offered a trial and, later, a position as a commis chef. His mother questioned why he would leave the relative security of Gary Rhodes for someone who does not accept anything less than the best. But in the food industry it is all about exposing oneself to experience in order to improve and, in 2000, Paul moved to Ramsay's flagship Royal Hospital Road restaurant in Chelsea. It was the next step and one that was essential in his development.

The F word is food

Still young at the age of 21, Paul had to take a slight demotion in order to enter the kitchen of his infamous new boss at Royal Hospital Road but that didn't seem to matter. His determination and strong work ethic drove him forward, and he remembers thinking: 'I am going to do this well and I am not leaving here unless I'm sacked.' Through a tough, pressurised environment, Gordon taught Paul to have great self-respect as well as respect for the profession and to have pride in the discipline and the difference that can be achieved by the *way* he worked.

Fighting through the pressure and the rigour, Paul continued to learn and after three successful years he started to think again about moving on. Knowing that Paul was considering moving to New York or working on cruise liners, Gordon put him forward for a job with his business partner at the time, Marcus Wareing. A sous chef position with Marcus would give Paul more responsibility, allowing him to work with suppliers and manage relationships with staff as well as cook. So in 2003 he started working for Marcus Wareing at Pétrus (now in Knightsbridge) and then, later, following him to The Berkeley. Working under Marcus was completely different from the ferocity of Gordon but equally rewarding, and Paul's passion for food and flavours really began to thrive. In terms of the industry, Paul's climb up the ladder had taken a relatively short space of time, with impressive mentors guiding him along the way, but this was not without immense effort and passion. After eight years, working 18-hour days and quite a few burnt limbs, Paul had established himself as a quality chef in a city full of food.

Lucky number 6

Throughout his career Paul has not been shy in tackling big challenges and taking the decisions that move him away from his comfort zone. In 2006 he left London and the security of big name mentors to take a more senior role at a restaurant in Kent. It quickly became apparent that this move was not everything Paul had anticipated but what could have reduced the young talent to another 'could-have been' actually opened the door to a fantastic professional opportunity in the meeting of an ex-colleague's father.

Derek Mapp, a successful entrepreneur who started the 52-strong Tom Cobleigh pub chain, was introduced to Paul through his son, the former pastry chef at Pétrus. Derek immediately took an interest in Paul's talent and made him a fairytale offer – to financially back Paul, his son and another former Pétrus 'graduate' and allow them to move into their own restaurant and run the kitchen. With high prices making a move to London practically impossible, the beautiful Cornish town of Padstow was eventually decided upon. With the heavyweight presence of Rick Stein in the town already, and its availability of fresh ingredients (being on the coast and close to the countryside), Padstow 'was a no brainer and I thought I could make my mark here and do something'. A Georgian town house at 6, Middle Street was found to be a suitable venue and, with high hopes and enthusiasm, the four of them opened Number 6 in 2006.

His determination and strong work ethic drove him forward.

Shaky starts

As with any new business, expectation was high and the restaurant represented something different for everyone involved, particularly for Paul and his two friends who wished to showcase the best of their culinary abilities early on. Hindsight now shows that the menu was probably too ambitious and convoluted to be sustained throughout the year – successful with tourists but alien to the locals. It was clear that, financially, things were looking bleak. 'We lost money every year for three years and it became more and more strenuous.' With things not going as well as they hoped and the strain beginning to show, Paul's two friends began to lose interest and made moves towards backing out of the restaurant entirely. Paul was

Moving to Padstow enabled Paul to work with fresh ingredients and challenge himself in a new venture.

suddenly faced with a monumental decision ... to stay in Padstow and try to turn it around or go.

Once again, Derek offered up the solution. With unshakeable belief that Paul could rework Number 6 into a successful restaurant, Derek offered him the chance to buy the lease and become sole owner. In 2009, a time when the recession was hitting food establishments all over the UK, taking on the project could be considered to be foolhardy. It would have been so much easier to return to London or Southampton and try something there but for Paul this was a once-in-a-lifetime opportunity.

Paul Ainsworth at . . .

To say it was tough would be an understatement but equally Paul acknowledges that 'nothing is for free and there is no easy road. There will be the odd success story that does it overnight, but for most it's hard work.' With the restaurant rebranded as Paul Ainsworth at Number 6 in January 2010, the pressure to make it a success was enormous. From the very beginning there was the feeling of hitting the ground running and Paul was now on his own. Not only did he have to rework the menu to fit in with the local community and his ethos of natural but playful dishes, he also had to learn the ropes of the restaurant trade as a whole. Paul remained in his chef whites but now he also worked front of house, learnt about wines, chatted to the customers, dealt with suppliers and studied everything about his business, with invaluable and impartial help from Derek.

The restaurant has now been rebranded as Paul Ainsworth at Number 6.

Even with interest rates plummeting, it was a hard start to owning a business and for six months he wasn't able to pay himself, meaning his wife's wage had to support them both. His sole concern was the restaurant: paying the staff, satisfying the customers and keeping things running. It would have been easy to quit during those first months but 'if you want your own business or something else, then it is bloody hard work, but don't give up' and he remained confident in his strategy of good cooking in a relaxed and unpretentious environment.

Paul acknowledges that 'nothing is for free and there is no easy road. There will be the odd success story that does it overnight, but for most it's hard work'.

Fortunately (and deservedly) Paul's hard work, philosophy of 'everyone welcome' and value for money quickly began to win out over complex dishes and expensive ingredients. Paul Ainsworth at Number 6 was branded by Lee Trewhela of *The Cornish Guardian* as 'the most outstanding dining experience in Cornwall' and with reviews like that and a revitalised reputation, the restaurant went from strength to strength. Number 6 has been consistently rated within the prestigious *Good Food Guide* since 2006, and the rebranded Paul Ainsworth at Number 6 was voted number 69 of the top 100 restaurants in the UK by the National Restaurant Awards 2011 and selected as one of The Good Food Guide's Top 50 UK Restaurants 2013, sitting at number 47. In late 2012, Paul Ainsworth at Number 6 was awarded the elusive accolade every chef dreams of, that golden Michelin star. After seven years in Padstow, Paul's culinary skills were now firmly on the map.

Expansion

In May 2010, once Paul had established Paul Ainsworth at Number 6, he and Derek got together once more to collaborate on a new venture. The Padstow Italian institution, Rojano's, was coming up for sale and with a great location just off the harbour. The two men decided it would make great business sense to buy the restaurant, 'it was too good an opportunity to miss'. Though Paul decided to remain at Number 6, where his name sits above the door, he was heavily involved once again in the renovation of the new restaurant, wanting to preserve its reputation while making his mark.

In recognition of the man who gave him his first break and influenced his career, Paul renamed the restaurant Rojano's in the Square, taking inspiration from the place where it all began, Gary Rhodes in the Square. He reworked the menu once more, taking his passion for simple Italian cooking and (though he doesn't work there) spending time with the chefs in order to train and teach them the new dishes. Opening in March 2011 with brand new owners and a brand new look, Rojano's in the Square represented both the expansion and dichotomy of Paul in Padstow – the high-end cuisine to the rustic family fare and the chef to the businessman.

Paul was asked to appear on BBC show *The Great British Menu* in 2011.

The great British chef

In 2011, one of Paul's staff walked into his office 'like he took these calls all the time' and handed him the phone with a '*The Great British Menu* are on the phone'. Among chefs and those who work in the industry, this BBC programme is the most respected and viewed. For each series, 24 of the country's top chefs are selected to compete regionally, and then nationally, in the bid to win one of the four courses at a prestigious banquet. With previous winners serving the Queen, returning British troops from Afghanistan and local suppliers and Prince Charles, there is fierce competition to win a place. While other shows might attract large audiences, there is none that Paul or his peers would rather win.

Receiving the final accepting phone call while on holiday in Rome, it did not take long for Paul to begin planning his menu. From that moment he was lost to his wife and any hopes for enjoying their trip. It became an obsession, for being chosen as one of the three top chefs to represent the South-West was an enormous compliment to someone relatively new to seeing his name above the door of a restaurant.

The 2011 competition focused on the community and celebrating the people who bring communities together through food. The Fisherman's Mission in Penzance and the Padstow RNLI inspired Paul's menu and drove his passion to win. After beating the heavyweight chefs of his region, newcomer Paul went on to compete against the other regional winners for a course at the final banquet. In the last round his impressive and interactive dessert, 'Taste of the Fairground', was chosen to be served to 100 guests at London's Leadenhall market. Paul's name, much like the mentors of his career, was now catapulted into the realms of media chefs.

Building upon experience

The contest brought out an explanation about the complex relationship with fate and hard work that has always pervaded Paul's career. He sees himself as a hard worker who has not necessarily been blessed with luck in competitions, although recognising that he has 'had luck in different areas', and concluding that 'luck is luck, but you make your own as well'. While circumstance has given Paul many opportunities, from working with Gary Rhodes to a chance to appear on such a respected show, it is only his own talent, dedication and discipline that has turned these events into successes. It seems to summarise so much of what his career has contained.

'Luck is luck, but you make your own as well.'

A second appearance on the *Great British Menu* in 2012, though not quite so successful, meant that Paul has stayed on the media radar. Though initially unsure of the role television would play within his catering career, there's no doubting that it has boosted his profile with the British public. However, maintaining links with his local suppliers and customers still come first and foremost. Despite the draw of celebrity chef status, Paul's trade, his business and his restaurants are still the most important thing. They 'are what will always be there and build a solid foundation for me, my wife, and eventually when I have a family.'

CHILDREN'S POET AND AUTHOR

Michael Rosen

Current title: author and visiting professor of children's literature at Birkbeck University

Age and DOB: 66 (b. 1946)

First job: professional 'chicken plucker' (for a Christmas holiday in his teens)

Other careers: radio and television broadcaster, lecturer and performer

Most well known for: Children's Laureate (2007-2009)

Hailed by critic Morag Styles as 'one of the most significant figures in contemporary children's poetry', Michael Rosen has been entertaining children and adults alike for over 35 years with his humorous and heartfelt poetry. His chatty, observational style was immediately successful in taking the 'stuffiness' out of traditional poetry and making it accessible to children by drawing on experiences they relate to and written in a language they understand. Michael has written and contributed to over 140 books and has been awarded many prizes for his works, none more prestigious than the two-year post of Children's Laureate in 2007. He is a recognised television and radio broadcaster, regularly hosting *Word of Mouth* on BBC Radio 4, as well as lecturing at universities on the subject of children's literature, actively promoting the use of poetry within education and performing his works in schools and libraries.

Early years

Born in 1946 in Middlesex, as the youngest son of Harold and Connie Rosen, Michael grew up in a world of literature and language. As part of a family of strong 'Jewish East End tradition' with both parents as teachers who frequently spoke Yiddish, French, German, Latin and Russian at home, Michael embraced the idea 'that language was something malleable, that you could play with' from an early age. His parents 'filled the house with books' and were always reading, collecting recordings of writers and writing themselves. There 'wasn't a day that went by when there wasn't something languagey going on'.

Despite a strong passion for literature founded at home, Michael didn't like poetry very much at primary school. 'It was a bit like medicine, you were told that it was good for you, but it didn't taste very nice.' School poetry seemed mournful and was taught in a regimented, traditional fashion – a world away from the excitement and enthusiasm his parents had tried to create. It wasn't until secondary school that 'something fizzed' when he was introduced to dramatic dialogues and started to write his own poetry, satirising people he knew. Michael's influences stem from a love of D.H. Lawrence, Carl Sandburg and the opening pages of James Joyce's *Portrait of the Artist as a Young Man*. In the sixth form he caught the Gerard Manley Hopkins 'bug' and attempted to imitate his work, with 'incomprehensible and boring' results.

It could have been so different . . .

It looked certain that his future would lie in literature when Michael went to sixth form to study English, French and History but there was something niggling at the back of his mind. The discovery of Jonathan Miller, a trained physician and prominent actor/director in the 1960s, had a profound effect on the teenage Michael and he was drawn to emulate Miller's academic success and become 'a sciencey-artsy person' too. So with the support of his parents, Michael made steps towards a career in medicine and was accepted into Middlesex Hospital Medical School to study a First MB, the equivalent of science A levels. But for a young man brought up on Shakespeare and D.H. Lawrence, Michael became unhappy and quickly realised he wanted to return to his passion. Despite feeling pressure from his parents, who did not want him to give up medicine, Michael hatched a plan. Although he hadn't yet been accepted into Oxford University, he was confident he would get a place at the same Oxford college as his brother and then swiftly transfer back to English, easy!

After a year at Middlesex Hospital, Michael was accepted onto the physiology course at Wadham College, Oxford, and completed his first year before finally making the round trip back to English language and literature, beginning his degree in 1966. Utilising the freedom of university, Michael began toying with the idea of becoming an actor. He spent a lot of his time writing, acting and directing plays and even contributed poems to his mother's programme with BBC Schools Radio. During his holidays, his mother would often sit at the kitchen table with piles of poems, trying to find a way to link two together. Michael would rush upstairs, quickly compose something that could be used as a filler and present it to his mother – 'it was shameless nepotism!'

In 1968, his final year at Oxford, Michael won *The Sunday Times* Drama Award for his independent play, *Backbone*. As a result of the competition *Backbone* was performed in London's Royal Court Theatre, and, due to the prestige of the competition and performance space, was published by Faber in 1969. He recalls sitting in the audience at the Royal Court, watching his play being performed and 'not quite knowing why I was there' – an overwhelming achievement which was a far cry from the teenage 'whim' of a medical career.

Unexpected directions

As a successful student with an obvious flair for writing and performing, Michael graduated from Oxford and, after a rigorous series of 'hoop jumping', won a prestigious place on the BBC's graduate trainee scheme. During his time there he was heavily involved within education and children's television, presenting a show called WALRUS (Write And Learn, Read, Understand, Speak) and writing for a children's reading series called Sam on Boff's Island. Then in 1972, after nearly three years in the corporation, Michael was suddenly 'asked to go freelance' and was essentially sacked in spite of his popularity with some BBC departments. The motive behind this mysterious decision was eventually revealed by a journalist 12 years later as being entirely political; Michael 'was investigated by MI5 who said that I wasn't trustworthy enough to have a post with the BBC'. It was a very personal move that he never quite came to terms with because 'it wasn't as if I wanted to corrupt the masses with Marxist propaganda, I kept my political life, social life and work life separate and I just really wanted to find ways to make literature popular through television'. This rejection came as shock to the young graduate who, at the time, was unknowingly battling with an underactive thyroid condition and was left reeling that 'things didn't seem to be going as well as they were'.

It took nearly a year of Michael 'hawking poetry around' before someone closer to home took notice and offered him a lifeline.

For six to nine months after his dismissal, Michael 'goofed around not really knowing what to do' but was still determined to be involved in film and television. As a 26-year-old, he eventually found his way to the National Film School, where he studied directing and writing. It was during his three years there that he collated a set of poems from his 'big pile' written over seven years and looked to get published again. With exposure on BBC Schools Radio and some poems contributing to other programmes and books, Michael approached his previous publisher, Faber, confidently. Assuming his poems were for an adult audience it came as a surprise when Faber rejected it as adult fiction and suggested he try the children's department instead. 'The poems began life in my mind as a kind of faux naif – using the voice of a child to talk about childhood and relations with adults – intended for adults, at least that's what I thought I was doing!' The children's department at Faber also rejected the manuscript believing that 'children don't like poetry written from their point of view'. It took nearly a year of Michael 'hawking poetry around' before someone closer to home took notice and offered him a lifeline.

Getting that elusive deal

Margaret Meek, a colleague of his father's at the Institute of Education, saw his poetry and recommended them to an editor she knew. 'Margaret saw a lot of writer's first texts; she lectured in children's literature at the institute and so what she thought held a lot of weight and, fortunately, she backed my poems.' In the 1970s, the publishing world was not quite as stringent as it is today. Michael was lucky that someone was willing to support his career and introduce him to the right person – Margaret was his 'de facto agent'. 'Nowadays scarcely anybody gets published without an agent. It really is your first port of call – to convince an agent that what you're writing is good and worth pushing forward.'

Margaret handed Michael's manuscript to the children's editor, Pam Royds, at the small, independent publisher, André Deutsch. His style and fun lyrics hit the mark and in 1973 Pam commissioned the collection – it was the break Michael had eagerly been waiting for and the start of a long-standing professional relationship. With the contract signed, there was the small matter of making the poems come to life, creating illustrations to capture the child's imagination. Michael firmly maintains that he is 'absolutely rubbish at drawing' so Pam paired his manuscript with an illustrator she had just finished working with, the incredible Quentin Blake. With a delay of just 18 months for the illustrations to be completed, the manuscript was ready for print. So in 1974, at the age of 28, Michael's first children's book *Mind Your Own Business* was published and he was primed to face the world of children's literature.

Embracing children's literature

Upon the publication of his first collection and finishing at the National Film School, Michael had to find ways of earning a living aside from poetry. 'I was sort of arrogant enough to think I could do it, make a living from books, but it was slightly complicated by the fact I had my first child and was thinking "oh blimey this is serious!"' So in 1976 he took up as writer in residence at the Vauxhall Manor Comprehensive School. A writer-in-residence programme is usually funded by the school or organisation they are involved with and it allows authors to develop their own work alongside creating projects, giving presentations and collaborating with pupils and staff as a way of raising the profile of literature. Though few and far between nowadays, these residencies do still exist and Michael relished the idea that 'you could get these residencies and then also fill up the week with performances, publishing, writing and so on. I suddenly thought "yeah this works, I could do this".'

Despite great support and enthusiasm from André Deutsch, Michael learnt that 'publishers don't really promote poetry' actively and so he had to find unique ways of getting his poems out to children. It was his fresh approach to self-publicising that really got his name known – he was one of the first poets to make visits and perform to schools throughout the UK and internationally. 'I didn't realise that if you wrote a children's book that there was this world, particularly in the seventies, where they wanted what I had. They wanted me to come into schools and libraries and book groups to read the poems so suddenly, whoosh, I was off! I was personally dealing with bookings all the time and I was just over the moon.'

Michael was one of the first poets to make visits and perform to schools throughout the UK and internationally.

Michael has always seen performing his work to children as key to his success.

Michael has always been driven to re-assert interest in poetry, particularly in children to whom it has become just another SAT question. 'I remember walking past a playground of a school I had been to a week before and the children all rushed to the fence and said, "Oh look! There's the poet! There's the poet", and I just remember being overcome. I couldn't have dreamt that something as lovely as that could have happened to me. I remember thinking that this is just heaven, basically, and that feeling remains. If someone had told me when I was 18, 21 that that was what it would be like for you, even now getting recognised in my sixties, I would have just said "yeah right!" (not that we had invented the phrase "yeah right!") but I just wouldn't have believed that things like that would happen through a combination of what I've done.'

Everyone's a critic . . .

In spite of his success with audiences, in the 1980s Michael started getting criticised by a small group within his own community. Several influential people began publishing their ideas and labelling Michael's work as 'mere entertainment', announcing that he had 'betrayed the craft of poetry'. Though Michael's approach and style were clearly popular, fundamentally his poetry was not written to serve the commercial masses. There was something a lot deeper in his work that he felt his critics were missing. 'I was saying something about power relationships between children and adults. There was seriousness under the humour and I felt at the time "well isn't that apparent?"!'

Michael freely admits that 'as a body of writing, my work is a rag-bag of styles and genres' and he acknowledges that by choosing not to write in traditional, perfected forms of poetry it may have isolated him as a target for critics. However, that was precisely the point. He was 'perfecting an oral voice, which actually requires another kind of craft' – he intended his poetry to be read out loud and performed as a way of breaking down the 'seriousness' of poetry for children. By choosing a different way of displaying rhymes, meter and couplets Michael attracted both negative and positive attention but 'when you're in the arts and you're trying to justify yourself, particularly if you say "look I am very serious and this is why I do this", people get annoyed quite quickly. So I stopped trying to justify myself through counter-articles and thought "well I'll just keep on writing" and he adopted the stance of "if you don't like my 'poetry' then just call it "stuff"'!

Diversity is key

Since 1973 Michael Rosen has been heavily involved in the writing and promotion of children's literature but his success within the genre and experiences presenting within the media have opened doors for him to explore 'a patchwork' of other things. Variety is one way Michael keeps his work fresh: 'there's something about me, maybe a certain restlessness or lack of self-belief almost, but I think that I want to keep trying lots of different ways of writing … my way is to write in lots and lots of different ways.'

Famed for poetry collections such as *You Wait Til I'm Older Than You* (1996) and *Uncle Billy Being Silly* (2001), Michael has also used his reputation and literary ability to diversify into other genres of children's literature. He has compiled anthologies, most notably *Culture Shock* (1990), created the narration for picture books, adapted folk stories and written two non-fiction books on Shakespeare and Dickens. In the adult market, he is a regular contributor to *The Guardian*, writes articles and books aimed at teachers who wish to incorporate poetry in their classrooms and has written anthologies of poetry based on three separate periods of difficulty in his life: *Carrying the Elephant* (2002); *That's Not My Nose* (2004) and *In The Colonie* (2005). In the world of literature alone, he has written or contributed to well over 140 different books, and he shows no sign of slowing down. He continues to work primarily with André Deutsch but has also collaborated with some big names in publishing, such as Penguin, Hodder Children's and Walker Books. Michael's method of securing book deals hasn't changed much since *Mind Your Own Business* – he still sends manuscripts on spec to commissioning editors but this time an agent pays for the postage.

His success within the genre and experiences presenting within the media have opened doors for him to explore 'a patchwork' of other things.

Inheriting an interest in the construction of language from his parents, Michael's television and radio programmes also tend to centre on the exploration of literature and language. His reputation as an orator and avid passion for the spoken word meant that he was the prime candidate to present new programmes. Often approached by writers and directors, Michael's voice has consequently become as recognisable as his poems. A presenter of BBC Radio 4's *Word Of Mouth* since 1998 – a programme that

Michael has contributed to over 140 books throughout his career to date.

looks at the English language and how it is used – Michael has frequented the airwaves on and off since 1970. A career highlight was his time presenting a programme for the BBC World Service called *Poems by Post* where people all over the world would write in with their favourite poems and Michael would give some background information on the poet and origin. 'I remember going into work and thinking "this is just about the most lovely, thrilling thing to do – to talk about poems and poets and have millions of people all over the world involved – blimey this is heaven"!'

Being a poet, even one who has reached the heights that Michael has, does not provide a single, workable income on its own so he positions himself in many guises in order to mix things up – one day he can be presenting and the next he can be picking up essays for his job as a university lecturer – but whatever he does, his world is firmly centred in language and literature. 'I have, very luckily, built up a sort of repertoire of jobs which are all pretty much language or performance-based but aren't the same.'

Awards and accolades

The ingeniousness and unique quality of Michael's 'stuff' (despite some early criticism) has led to high recognition and praise throughout his time in the literary world. One of the books most synonymous with Michael is his collaboration with illustrator Helen Oxenbury *We're Going on a Bear Hunt* – a charming family adventure story based on an old American camp song – which has won many international awards, including the 1989 Nestlé Smarties Book Prize. Michael has also been short-listed for the Kate

Greenaway Prize and the Carnegie Medal, and in 1997 he received the Eleanor Farjeon Award for his contribution and commitment to children's literature. However, his greatest accolade was yet to come.

In 2007, it was announced that Michael would be appointed the fifth Children's Laureate. This prestigious two-year post is awarded to an established writer or illustrator who has made significant contributions to the field of children's literature. Michael was the first poet to receive the honour. 'It was such an immense privilege because you were judged by your peers, it's a group of people who are in the business saying, "we think you could do this for two years"'. During his two years as Laureate Michael embraced the opportunity to raise the profile of poetry in classrooms and the media, a cause he feels most passionately about. Wanting to release poetry from the 'National Curriculum strait-jacket' of counting adjectives and finding metaphors, Michael worked hard to reignite the trend of performing poetry in classrooms. He created The Poetry Friendly Classroom, an online resource to be used by teachers, which provides video tips, activity sheets and general advice, and set up the complementary website Perform-a-Poem which features video poems made by young people all over London. He also inaugurated the Roald Dahl Funny Prize, an annual award for authors of humorous children's fiction that aims to promote laughter as a feel-good factor in children's fiction.

Making it in the industry and staying there

Even now there is a factor of trial and error when it comes to being published; past successes don't guarantee the next book contract. 'You must think of yourself as being more productive than you are received and that's fine! If you think in terms of an actor who has to repeatedly rehearse and rehearse – no one sees the rehearsal except the director. Writers have to have a system of monitoring what they're doing and accepting what people are saying to you about your stuff, not just assume that because you've written something that it's good enough.'

Michael uses performances to try new material and create new concepts.

Michael utilises every opportunity to write, even taking a turn towards the modern world of social media and using it as yet another medium to work and practise styles in. 'My way is to write in lots and lots of different ways, that's why I'm excited by Twitter and Facebook and blogging, it's a completely other type of writing. It's brilliant! You can write a 140-character poem or write an article about the most serious issue of the day or write a jokey entry on Facebook. I'm very intrigued by the idea that writing is malleable.'

He also uses performances to try new material and create new concepts. 'I see it as a sort of stand-up comedy where I make up new bits and sometimes, just from me mucking around, I've got a new poem.'

There is a firm acknowledgement that nowadays there is no alternative but to throw oneself head first into work if aiming to succeed in the saturated market of children's fiction, especially within poetry. 'If you write poems, they will not sell themselves. You have to get yourself into schools, into youth groups – whatever it is – just get in and keep doing it day in, day out so that people slowly discover your work. When I see people younger than me who are doing very well, like Jacob Sam-La Rose and Valerie Bloom, it's because they're working hard – Valerie is in schools every day of the week!' There seems to be no allowance for sitting at home with your feet up within fiction, even at 66 Michael is still out there working with his audiences. 'If I didn't I know my books will go out of print, that is the way of the world. If you don't put yourself out there you will slip off the dial within six months, there is just too much other stuff out there.'

CLASSICAL MUSICIAN

Joshua Bell

Current title: violinist and director of the Academy of St Martin's in the Fields

Age and DOB: 44 (b. 1967)

First job: 'it's always been music'

Other careers: teaching, conducting and directing

Most well known for: *Washington Post* viral stunt

In the world of classical music, numerous labels have been ascribed to Joshua Bell: prodigy, virtuoso and genius are but a few. He is renowned not only for his energetic performances and mastery of his instrument but for his boyish good looks and willingness to adapt the classical and embrace the contemporary.

In essence, Joshua is more than just a musician. He has released 36 records and won both the Grammy Award and Mercury Prize. He is America's greatest violinist, and arguably one of the world's greatest classical musicians. How is this all possible, you may ask? The answer is simple. Make your passion your career.

Formative years

Joshua's first violin lesson was at the tender age of four, after his parents noticed him plucking tunes with elastic bands he had stretched over the handles of his dresser drawer. These early lessons allowed him to explore his musical curiosity from a young age, although at this stage the violin was nothing more than an outlet for his childhood creativity. Looking at Joshua's early childhood doesn't reveal anything out of the ordinary, with the minor exception that his parents considered music a key educational subject holding as much weight as English, science or mathematics. This being said, they encouraged him in all aspects of his life, including sports. Joshua showed some talent for tennis as a youngster, winning state competitions and even going on to participate in national-level finals.

Joshua notes that his parents were always searching for the best teachers and those who would challenge him: 'I'm grateful to my parents for always being my advocate in that department.' He speaks highly of his various violin teachers and stresses the importance of their role in his early formation. Each of his teachers provided him with varying and unique experiences, which have shaped the man he is today.

Each of Joshua's teachers provided him with varying and unique experiences that have shaped the man he is today.

Joshua showed a talent for the violin from a very early age.

Fine tuning

Joshua's first violin lessons instilled in him a joy for music and he delighted in playing his violin. However, his second violin teacher, Mimi Zweig, was meticulous in forcing him to go back to basics and hone his technical skills on the instrument. Shortly afterwards, at the age of 11, Joshua attended the Meadowmount School for Strings summer camp run by Ivan Galamian, who was considered one of the best musical teachers in the USA at the time. Joshua had obtained a place on the prestigious camp by auditioning with a tape recording. As a young boy he was still used to slotting his music practice into his daily schedule without much cause for disturbance. However, the camp required a rather gruelling schedule of five hours' practice a day. This gave him the structure he needed to further his education musically. More importantly, it proved to be the catalyst Joshua needed to find his passion and begin to pursue his dreams, having fallen in love with the violin.

Joshua's first music recital was soon to follow at the age of 12. Amazingly Joshua's career may not have got underway at this point thanks to an incident prior to the recital. Joshua recalls that 'the day of my first solo recital I was tossing around a boomerang which whirled back and sliced my chin open. Two inches to the left and I couldn't have held my violin. But I played, wounded.' Josef Gingold, who had also been a teacher at the music camp and an exceedingly reputable violin professor from Indiana University, was in the audience. He was so impressed by the performance that he agreed to mentor the young Joshua. Gingold was to become his most important pedagogue, with Joshua proclaiming him as the source of his own musical inspiration. 'What I loved about him was that he was not possessive as a teacher, in fact he told me to go play for this person and that person, he really wanted me to experience other points of view.'

Under the guidance of Gingold, Joshua began to study the violin at Indiana University while simultaneously continuing his normal school life at Bloomington High School North. Having found his direction early on, Joshua was determined to succeed. Nonetheless, it was no mean feat juggling music with school life. Joshua had to know how to manage his time and become efficient at learning so that he could accomplish everything he set out to achieve. Although he confesses that he occasionally sneaked out of his violin practices to play computer games for a couple of hours before rushing back in time for his mother to pick him up.

Joshua had to know how to manage his time and become efficient at learning so that he could accomplish everything he set out to achieve.

Joshua's first big break came at the age of 14 when he won a General Motors/*Seventeen* magazine competition, which was a competition exclusively for young American high school musicians. Joshua was selected for the competition from his audition tape. He then had to perform against a flutist and a pianist, both much older than him. Joshua won the grand prize, which gave him the chance to perform with the Philadelphia Orchestra and conductor Ricardo Muti. He was the youngest ever performer to play with the orchestra, and this created a fair amount of press attention, resulting in a guest appearance on *The Today Show*.

Hamlen-Landau Management had also watched his Philadelphia performance. The company approached Joshua's parents after the concert with the hope of launching and nurturing his career, but his mother remembers that 'as parents we weren't that interested in having anyone take over his life at that point, after all he was still only 14'. Joshua stayed in contact with Hamlen-Landau and a year later signed with them. It was a small, friendly company that looked after the young Joshua with care, allowing his parents to travel with him to various performances.

The gaining of management 'set everything on course' for Joshua. It was these early teen years that saw him grow and flourish through hard work and a determination to master his craft, enabling him to take on such challenging professional roles at a tender age. Consequently Joshua graduated from Bloomington High school, aged 16, in 1984, ready to embark on a three-week European tour, going to show that those who are goal-driven and have the passion can achieve fantastic things even while studying at school.

The key is variance

Since his first tour, Joshua has travelled the globe and performed with the world's finest musicians, conductors and orchestras. Some of Joshua's global success comes from his signing to the record label London Decca Records in 1986 at just 18 years of age. The label approached Joshua as it was eager to promote him as a contemporary and fresh-faced starlet of the classical world who would appeal to a mass market. This angle worked and Joshua's music video even appeared on the popular music channel VH1.

Joshua produced 14 albums with Decca before moving to Sony Classical in 1996. However, it is clear from the manner in which Joshua talks about music, that his true artistic talent and dedication shines through. He strongly believes the idiomatic mantra that one is one's own worst critic but says this is important when aiming to continually improve and strive for perfection.

A close look at Joshua's career to date shows he has achieved a staggering amount, but he is quick to warn that 'you can't do everything fully, you have to be able to make choices in life'.

'You can't do everything fully, you have to be able to make choices in life.'

Joshua further attests to the fact that variety is key to continued happiness and job satisfaction. He has been unafraid of forays into other styles and genres, maintaining that this is vital in order to keep things fresh and exciting. Joshua has experimented with jazz, Latin and also bluegrass music on the album *Short Trip Home*. It is these kinds of musical collaborations which tested his versatility. He had to be flexible and adapt to challenges such as working with a musician who doesn't traditionally read music (Sam Bush on *Short Trip Home*).

Similarly Joshua hasn't shied away from working with more contemporary popular musicians. The album *At Home with Friends* saw him collaborate with artists including Josh Groban, Sting and Christen Chenoweth. He notes that the advantage of such cross-over projects allow him to expose

Joshua has experimented with a number of different genres and styles of music.

people to classical music who might otherwise not have a particular interest, while simultaneously expanding his own fan base. Moreover, it gave Joshua an opportunity to compose, something he is keen to add to his burgeoning résumé. Joshua and pianist Frankie Moreno took 'Eleanor Rigby' and turned it into a more complex classical version with beautiful harmonies and delicate intricacies. It is exactly this kind of willingness to adapt and experiment which has earned Joshua a rightful place as one of the greatest violinists alive today.

Joshua has also been fortunate enough to contribute his talents to film scores. Most notably he was accredited as playing 'like a god' on the Oscar-winning score for *The Red Violin*. Francois Girard (the director of the film) approached Joshua after a concert in London. The pair talked about a possible film score for Joshua. They then became friends as well as collaborative colleagues on the film itself.

Leadership and technology

Now in his early forties, Joshua has begun to take on more and more challenging roles. His latest venture has seen him become the director of the London-based Academy of St Martin in the Fields. The pressure was certainly on him as he is only the second person to hold the title and the first American. Joshua had played with the orchestra before and gleefully accepted their offer of the role when it was proposed to him. The group is touring globally together and this is a big step for Joshua in terms of tackling more demanding leadership-based projects.

Joshua notes: 'being in charge of the overall concept, how I convey that and get the best results is a skill I am still refining'. In order to conduct the orchestra while still playing his violin, Joshua leads them from his concert-master chair and occasionally waves his bow like a baton. In taking up this new role, Joshua has had to adapt to the challenge of being both performer and conductor. He admits the hard work has already been done in the rehearsals, where it was necessary for him to have a strong hand, as he had to take on the views of those around him in terms of creativity, but maintain his own ideas for direction. Thus, during the performance Joshua knows when he is needed as leader and gives clear instruction while focusing on his own individual performance. He remarks: 'finding a balance between maintaining their respect and being their friend is hard but it can be done'.

The classical music world tends to be either sceptical or suspicious of technological advancement. As an avid computer game fan, Joshua is extremely open-minded when it comes to the worlds of technology and music colliding as they inevitably do in the 21st century. For example in January 2012, he took part in a concert with pianist Sam Haywood, where technology played a prominent role. Instead of the traditional human page-turner and sheet music, Haywood performed with the aid of an iPad2, complete with Bluetooth foot pedal to turn the pages. Joshua is impartial to the use of this type of device, noting that technology must not take away or distract from the performance. However, the benefits of such a device are clear, with apps available that enable access to large databases of music scores in the public domain and the ability for pages to be annotated via user interaction. Overall, he is pleased that technology and music are coming together and foresees a future where technology will continue to aid music development.

Technology has also been responsible for gaining Joshua greater media exposure. He has become unwittingly infamous for a *Washington Post* experiment in 2007, which saw him performing incognito in the Washington D.C. metro station. Journalist Gene Weingarten was awarded the Pulitzer Prize for his article's analysis of the experiment addressing the role of context in artistic perception, with arguably America's greatest violinist being largely ignored by passing commuters. A video of the stunt went viral with over 3.5 million views to date, gaining Joshua swathes of publicity.

However, Joshua does take his position in the classical music world seriously and tasks himself as a leader of tomorrow. In 2002, he became adjunct professor at Massachusetts Institute of Technology Media Lab. When asked to participate in projects involving music and children Joshua jumped at the chance. He assisted the development of new musical instruments and toys that help engage and facilitate the learning of music among children. Although Joshua is in no hurry to trade in his Stradivarius for an electric violin he sees the value in developing new ideas, especially if they inspire children to have an appreciation for music.

Joshua is aware of this need to foster a positive attitude towards music for future generations. He is also an advisory board member for the charity programme Education Through Music (ETM), which promotes integration of music into schools catering to disadvantaged children so as to enrich their learning. Joshua attends a number of schools and gives his time to conduct classes and speak to children about music. He says that 'getting kids interested in music and just exposed to it at an early age is something very important to me'.

A day in the life and final advice

When asked what a typical day entails, Joshua remarked: 'there really isn't a typical day. That is why I love my job. Every day is different.' It's clear that the life of a professional musician is one determined by a strict touring and recording schedule which leaves time for little else, not to mention the time spent on publicity and promotion. A new day sometimes even means a new city. Joshua copes with this constant movement by introducing elements of routine into his schedule. On the day of a concert he likes to prepare himself and 'lay low'. He eats pasta in his dressing room to give him energy for his high-octane performances and conducts slow – almost meditational-type – practising, so that he doesn't lose his energy. The key to this type of preparation is to stay calm and focused because 'when I walk out on stage I'm just ready and focused to give everything, I don't hold anything back and you have to set yourself up to do that'.

'When I walk out on stage I'm just ready and focused to give everything, I don't hold anything back and you have to set yourself up to do that.'

In terms of advice for aspiring musicians Joshua feels performance is paramount. He strongly advises musicians to take every performance opportunity as and when they arise saying 'you learn most from experience and getting up on stage and playing'. He feels that too many people are too choosy about their performances, and that if you are just starting out you can't 'turn your nose up at some small venue or dinky orchestra'. Joshua likens his career to a journey. 'I don't know exactly where I am going but I follow my instincts. Certain projects come along that I never thought I would do and that leads to other things'. As with any career there are particular tasks or moments that lead to frustration and annoyance. When asked how he coped with these darker days, Joshua said: 'I would have bad days or even bad weeks where I thought "my God I'm terrible", the funny thing is those bad weeks are usually followed by big breakthroughs, so I learnt not to despair.' Regarding what the pinnacle of his career has been, Joshua remarked, 'I haven't got there yet, I hope it is yet to come. There have been some great moments like playing in Carnegie Hall.'

Joshua feels that teachers and positive relationships with them are a vital starting point to a musical career. He advises learning to take every opportunity that comes and to ensure leading a varied and well-rounded existence so that during moments of frustration, it is easier to step away and refocus one's efforts. Joshua feels that 'in life as a musician it's very important to keep yourself challenged, for me that's now directing and composing'. It is clear from Joshua's case that having goal-driven commitments to succeeding enables achieving extraordinary results.

COMPOSER

Eric Whitacre

Current title: composer, conductor, lecturer

Age and DOB: 42 (b. 1970)

First job: appearing in a McDonald's advert

Other careers: teaching

Most well known for: forming the virtual choir

At the age of 18, Eric Whitacre had a passionate desire to be an electropop star, although he was unable to read music and had a firm belief that choir singing was 'geeky'. Yet just two years later, as a music undergraduate, Eric was amazing audiences with his very own classical compositions. Now aged 42, Eric is a multi-award-winning classical composer who, with the help of YouTube and 2,945 singers from across the globe, has propelled classical music into the 21st century. While Eric may have discovered his passion later than one might expect, once he had found it he was not prepared to let the fears of his parents or the criticism of teachers hold him back. 'If you want to do something, if you truly want to do it, then you just don't let anyone talk you out of it.'

Growing up in Nevada

Growing up in a small farming town in Nevada, USA, Eric has never received any formal musical training. His introduction to performing came at the age of 14 when, unable to read music, he played the trumpet by ear in his school concert band. However, at this age Eric's true passion lay with sound synthesisers, rather than with wind instruments.

'If you want to do something, if you truly want to do it, then you just don't let anyone talk you out of it.'

In 1984, Eric appeared in a McDonald's advert, after responding to a radio commercial announcing the opening. With the royalties from this work, he was able to buy his very own synthesiser and from then on became determined to follow in the footsteps of his favourite electropop band, Depeche Mode. Eric remained true to his dream of being a pop sensation throughout high school, where he played the synthesiser in his own pop band until leaving to attend the University of Nevada at the age of 18.

Once there, 'astonished to find that there was no degree programme offered for future popstars', Eric decided to major in music, as it seemed the best idea until he 'hit the big time'. In the meantime, Eric was asked to join the choir by choral conductor, David Weiller, an offer which he first declined as he believed choir people were 'geeky'. However, persuaded by the number of attractive female sopranos, Eric eventually joined – a move that would change his musical passion and his life forever.

The choir years

In the first session, the choir sang Mozart's *Requiem* and Eric was instantly mesmerised by the beauty of the piece and the enthusiasm of the choirmaster: 'It was like seeing colour for the first time. I became a choral geek of the highest magnitude.' Aware that this was a defining moment, Eric informed his parents of his new passion, but his enthusiasm was not met with encouragement. 'They never thought that I was going to make it as a pop star but I think that they were even more concerned when I came home and declared that I had fallen in love with choral music.'

Despite concerns that Eric's new passion may not give him a very stable career, Eric's parents have always been incredibly supportive of his career choice.

Eric had experienced an overwhelming sensation at his choir lessons and he knew that this was more than just a craze. Undeterred, he continued to attend choir rehearsals, where he was regularly moved to tears, and in his second year, he was accepted into the advanced choir. Eric had been learning to read music for the past year and despite not yet feeling quite comfortable with the skill, he decided to compose a piece of music for his choirmaster, as a mark of gratitude for his inspiring teaching. Set to 'Go Lovely Rose', a poem by Edmund Waller, the piece was completed in 1991 and sung by the choir in the finale to the Western Regional American Choral Directors Association (ACDA) in the Spring of 1992, where it was a huge success.

Eric had been learning to read music for the past year and despite not yet feeling quite comfortable with the skill, he decided to compose a piece of music for his choirmaster, as a mark of gratitude for his inspiring teaching.

The ACDA is a non-profit music education organisation, which aims to promote excellence in choral music. Attended by hugely influential people in the industry, this was a big break for Eric, who was at this time still an undergraduate. Remarkably, despite being Eric's first attempt at choral composition, 'Go Lovely Rose' impressed Barbara Harlow of Santa Barbara Music so much that she approached Eric after the performance and informed him that she wished to publish his piece. Eric agreed to write two more songs to flower poems, to create a set for the music publisher, who would manage the commissions and help him promote his work.

Yet, Eric's overwhelming passion for classical music did not end with choral compositions and in 1993, Eric was awe-struck by the power of the university wind symphony, after overhearing a rehearsal by the group, which consisted of six percussionists and eight trumpeters. Ever-determined to push himself, Eric immediately set on the idea of creating his own wind composition, despite having no prior experience of writing for instruments. After focusing on his challenge throughout the Christmas break, Eric presented 'Ghost Train' to the conductor of the wind symphony at the beginning of the new year and it was played at the College Band Directors National Association Convention in the following spring. This was another amazing opportunity for Eric as the convention, which aims to help university students looking for a career in the wind music industry, was heavily attended by useful contacts.

Once again, the piece met with an explosive response and at just 25 years old, Eric suddenly found he had band composers ringing him at home, requesting to buy his music. However, this time Eric opted to retain copyright to his work and he remains grateful of this decision today, as it meant that he would not have to split the profits from commissions with a publishing company. 'This decision made all the difference in the world. It allowed me to actually start making a living as a composer – otherwise I never would have.' Soon Eric began receiving direct commissions for his work, marking the beginning of his formal career as a freelance composer.

The degree years

Eric's professional career may have rapidly taken off, but he was still an undergraduate at the University of Nevada, where he was struggling to juggle his new occupation with his studies. Skipping lessons and failing classes, Eric strived for seven long years to gain his degree, but he was constantly held back by his tutors. 'By the end of it I was just so annoyed at the establishment. I was a professional composer, having my pieces played all over the place and yet because I'd failed to gain a few credits, they wouldn't let me leave.' Understandably, Eric grew tired of battling with his university requirements and decided to drop out of university in 1995. However, shortly afterwards, during a four-hour long discussion with a tutor named Dr Bruce Mayhall, he was persuaded to finish his degree.

So a few months later, Eric finally graduated from the University of Nevada and went straight on to study for a master's degree in composition at the reputable Juilliard School, again under the advice of Dr Mayhall. Before attending Juilliard, Eric had discovered a new depth to concert music, through the work of composers such as Stravinsky and he did not feel that he could make sense of such talent on his own. For this reason, he remains grateful to his 'amazing teacher' at Juilliard, Oscar-winning composer, John Corigliano, who helped Eric to make even better use of his creativity.

Despite this, Eric feels there are other routes to the top. 'I think that academia is a long and painful way to the top; it is hugely overrated as a means to success.' Despite attending Juilliard, as he believed that this was the correct pattern for someone interested in his line of work, Eric now feels that he should not have felt obliged to continue studying. 'I must have been 30 years old before I looked back and said actually I did not need to do all that. All I really needed to do was just sing in a choir and be around people who were passionate and smart.'

Nonetheless, Eric remains grateful for his time at both institutions, as although he feels he did not necessarily need the qualifications that he struggled to achieve over his nine years of study, it was at these establishments that he discovered his talent. Moreover, he is especially indebted to Dr Mayhall for persuading him to attend Juilliard, as it was here that he met his wife, soprano Hila Piltmann.

'All I really needed to do was just sing in a choir and be around people who were passionate and smart.'

A very brief stint at teaching

After graduating from Juilliard in 1997, Eric moved to Los Angeles and gained some teaching experience of his own in a private school, where he taught a range of choirs. Although he had by this point been receiving commissions for his work for a few years, at the age of 27 he was under pressure from his father to get a 'real job' with a steady income. However, teaching did not come easily to Eric and his composing had to take a temporary back seat, as his schedule did not allow time for it. Consequently, he only lasted at the school for one semester. 'The only good thing about that job was that it made me realise I had to make my composing career work. I didn't know what I was going to do, but obviously I couldn't cope with a real job. I felt like I was going to die if I couldn't make music.'

Having learnt that he could not always trust the advice of his teachers, Eric also discovered that his parents did not always know what was best either. 'Everyone's parents have an idea about what they should be doing and they mean well, but ultimately it's your life, you have to make the decisions.' Consequently, Eric made the firm decision that he was no longer going to strive to pacify his parents and he concentrated on doing what made him happy.

Making it happen

Determined to make a living out of his passion, Eric started dedicating all of his time to writing music from the second bedroom of his house and taking any commissions that came his way, irrespective of the pay, which would be decided following a mutual discussion. In 1999, a file-sharing website called Napster suddenly gave Eric's career the kick-start he had been hoping for and despite the free music website failing to make money for artists, it served to raise Eric's profile dramatically. By 2001, the website had closed due to infringement of copyright laws, but in that one year, Eric's compositions were being traded all over the internet.

Eric followed his new-found passion for music and made his dream of composing a reality.

The same year, Eric was asked by the ACDA to write the prestigious Raymond W. Brock commission, which was set up in 1991 as a memorial to the former ACDA administrative assistant. Along with poet Charles Antony Silvestri, Eric composed 'Leonardo Dreams of His Flying Machine' and remains the youngest composer to be honoured with the commission.

In the meantime Eric had spent any time that he was not composing contacting potential commissioners and seeking work. In 2003 he noticed that his hard work had paid off, as people had started to contact him. 'It was like I'd been pushing this snowball for so long and then suddenly, it seemed like overnight the snowball was working on its own. I didn't need to push anymore.'

By 2004 Eric had to hire an assistant just to handle the number of emails he was receiving and he could finally feel comfortable in the knowledge that he was making a sufficient living out of his talent. In 2005, Eric got his first manager and continued composing frantically until 2006, when a CD compilation of his work 'Cloudburst' and other choral works, was recorded by Polyphony and conducted by Stephen Layton, following discussions with his new manager. The CD was a huge success and went onto receive a Grammy nomination in best choral performance.

'It was like I'd been pushing this snowball for so long and then suddenly, it seemed like overnight the snowball was working on its own. I didn't need to push anymore.'

Breaking boundaries

In 2009, a young girl named Britlin Losee sent Eric a video of herself singing a track from his album, titled 'Sleep'. Taken aback by the beauty and innocence of her voice, Eric was struck with an idea. If he could get a group of people to sing the same song in soprano, alto, tenor or bass, it could be cut together as one piece. He recorded himself conducting his composition of 'Lux Aurumque' and after making the download to this piece free, he urged online fans to sing their part, according to their vocal range. Eric received videos from an astounding 185 singers and they were cut together and posted on YouTube to form Eric's first virtual choir. The response to the video was explosive and it received over a million hits in the first month. The virtual choir began as a 'cool' experiment for Eric, however, after listening to the power of the finished piece, he soon realised that something extremely special had been started.

Consequently, Eric decided to push his experiment to the next level. This time he decided to use the original song that Britlin Losee had performed to create Virtual Choir 2.0, setting a goal this time of 900 singers. Once all the videos had been received, the result far exceeded Eric's expectations and Virtual Choir 2.0 was eventually formed of 2,052 singers from 58 countries around the world. Previewed at TEDTalk, which showcases innovative projects in technology, entertainment and design, Virtual Choir 2.0 received the first full standing ovation of the conference.

Since discovering the amazing impact that the combination of music and modern technology could have on connecting people 'from as far North as Alaska and as far South as New Zealand', Eric has continued to test its limits. Virtual Choir 3.0 was released in April 2012 and combined the voices of 2,945 singers from 73 countries. Co-commissioned by Titanic Belfast and Northern Ireland Tourist Board, Virtual Choir 3.0 was projected onto the walls of the Titanic Belfast Visitor Centre at precisely 11:40pm on Saturday, 14 April 2012, to mark exactly 100 years since the *Titanic* hit the iceberg. While Virtual Choir 3.0 received support from generous partners, Eric has deliberately kept his three virtual choirs non-commercial, funding them largely between himself and his manager. Moreover, Eric asserts that this unifying force will be continued and he already has plans for Virtual Choir 4.0. 'It has an unbelievable momentum and I feel a responsibility to take all of this energy that we've created and harness it into something positive.'

Eric recorded himself conducting for his virtual choir.

Passion

Eric's virtual choirs serve as a testament to the power of modern technology and he hopes that his project will encourage aspiring composers to use social media to their benefit. 'If you can just create something original that speaks to people, then suddenly you've got your own little thing moving and YouTube, Facebook and Twitter are essential tools for that now.' Despite the multitudes of people attempting to get noticed on such sites, Eric insists that the greatest thing about composing is that you are not competing with anyone. 'You have the chance to concrete your own voice and your own style and kind of build your own corner of the world. All of my pieces are icons of my memories.'

Eric believes that the key to his success has been his determination to do exactly what makes him happiest. He explains that the idea of being a responsible adult and getting a job came very late to him: 'I am always very surprised when people are just 18 and know what they want to do with their lives', and consequently he believes that not having a set plan is not the end of the world. Despite being successful, he feels that this has been a secondary result of him simply following his passion. 'Still to this day I just feel like I'm doing what I love to do and all the rest has just fallen into place.' His virtual choir, he says, 'is the perfect example of something that I just thought was a cool idea, but it resulted in taking my career in directions I never could have imagined.'

Eric feels that his success has been a secondary result of him simply following his passion.

Throughout his career, Eric has challenged himself with many exciting new ventures such as writing the theme music for *Pirates of the Caribbean: On Stranger Tides*, and he has reaped the benefits of doing work that he enjoys. Among his many ventures is Eric's own musical, *Paradise Lost: Shadows and Wings*. Beginning with performances in California State University in 2003, the musical was eventually performed in the prestigious Carnegie Hall in 2010. The stage show, which combines a variety of musical genres, from opera to electronic, began as a venture shared between Eric and his friend.

However, Eric is determined not to let his creation die. 'I have become just so invested in it that it has become even more than a passion. It has become a test of my will against the universe.' *Paradise Lost: Shadows and Wings* is arriving in the UK for the first time in 2013, where it will be performed in the West End and Eric is unwavering in his determination to make it a success. 'I am going to make this work. I am going to make this happen.'

Setting new goals

Having experienced the unanticipated success of his virtual choir in 2010, Eric and his new manager, Claire Long, decided it was time to discuss how to build on the momentum of his achievement. After a consultation on strategy, Claire and Eric decided that the next objective would be to gain a recording contract with a major record company. Shortly after, Eric achieved his goal and signed a long-term multi-album contract with Decca as a performer, which meant that for the first time, he would conduct as well as compose all of the pieces. His first album with the record company, *Light and Gold*, was released in 2010 and became the number one classical album in both the UK and US charts within a week, before winning a Grammy Award in 2012.

Eric's second album with Decca, named *Water Night*, debuted at number one in the iTunes and Billboard classical chart after its release in 2012. The album cover features an image of Eric with 'three-day stubble', removing his bow tie: 'There's a move to try and sex things up and this time Decca decided to push that button. Not only am I mortified, I'm left thinking "Seriously, is anyone finding this sexy?"'

After struggling to establish an impressive reputation among the 'closed circle' of classical music artists, Eric was left feeling frustrated as the new album created an opening for the 'classical establishment' to criticise his work. 'They just look at it and think, "Look, this is exactly what we expected it to be" and then they punch really hard at it.' His music continues to sell well nonetheless, and Eric has had to accept that 'it's just classic record company stuff'.

A typical week

Between releasing award-winning albums and creating choirs of thousands, Eric's career does not allow for a standard week. In September 2011, Eric added to his mounting schedule when he agreed to a five-year appointment as composer-in-residence at the University of Cambridge – a position for which he was approached, following a visiting fellowship. Yet, despite the extra workload, Eric describes this as 'the dream'. With a job description that requires him to 'add to the cultural enrichment of the university', Eric is left to decide his own agenda. Some weeks, he may schedule in a lecture, or choir practice, while others he may just occupy a room in the university to write his compositions. Alongside occasionally lecturing at Cambridge, Eric often uses his skills of oration as a guest speaker at venues across the globe, including the Seoul Digital Forum and Harvard University.

His latest initiative, Soaring Leap, involves a series of workshops around the world, where he advises singers, composers and conductors. With a host of public appearances and his responsibility at Cambridge to attend to, Eric's career requires a great deal of travel from his home, which is currently in London. However, he remains committed to his passion and always insists on dedicating time solely to composing new work.

Alongside his many work commitments, Eric also finds time for his wife and their Six-year-old son. Eric's wife, Grammy Award-winning soprano, Hila Piltmann, has worked with her husband many times, including featuring in his album *Waternight*, and performing at the New York premiere of *Paradise Lost: Shadows and Wings*. Despite being a musical couple, Hila and Eric have no plans to force their son to do anything against his will. 'So far he thinks classical music is boring and we're not pushing it.'

Eric's entire success is founded on knowing when to follow his own dreams and ignore the concerns and criticisms of others. Once he had discovered what he wanted to do, he was not prepared to make compromises. 'If you have nothing to fall back on then you have to figure out how to make it work.' Despite throwing himself into composing with no set plan for the future, Eric's career fell into place and then exploded into directions he never could have dreamed possible. 'The only consistent thing in my career has been me doing what I love; everything else has just worked around that.'

CREATIVE DIRECTOR

Paul Brazier

Current title: creative director at AMV BBDO

Age and DOB: 49 (b. 1962)

First job: checkout operator at Sainsbury's

Other careers: illustrator

Most well known for: writing the Guinness adverts, top prizes at Cannes Lions and being elected President of D&AD

'I'm from a little place called Tipton in the West Midlands and I suppose it's known for steel works and so on. No ad-agencies around there. For someone like me, someone who isn't academically astute or driven, there isn't a lot.' So begins the narrative of Paul Brazier, Executive Creative Director of the biggest advertising agency in the country, AMV BBDO. If all of the campaigns he had worked on had his signature scrawled in their bottom corner, he would be a household name. BMW, Sainsbury's, Twinning's, Guinness, Cancer Research. But advertising is a different type of artistry and there are no exhibitions or retrospectives for the creatives. Still, art is very much the foundation for Paul's success.

'Let's start with the longest story I've got.'

Once serious ambitions to be a footballer were thwarted by an injury (even now he is gutted that he couldn't trial at West Brom because of it), Paul was forced to dream differently. He remembers one teacher saying to his mother, almost as if he wasn't there, 'at least he's got his art to fall back on', and thinking in reply 'God, I'm *that* crap'. Art didn't offer an easy route to a job and it certainly didn't come with a salary. Although he was talented in that he could draw, the best response this received was: 'maybe you can have some pictures framed and put on the wall, but meanwhile you have to become a lorry driver or join the army'. With that gloomy outlook and his footballing career over before it could start, Paul enrolled in an art foundation course. However, he did ensure he left school with some O levels, already thinking they would be necessary when he inevitably became a teacher.

His teachers recognised that he was talented and encouraged him, but repeatedly ignored his question of 'what do you think I'll do?'. When they revealed that they saw him as a sculptor, a fine artist like they were, Paul twisted away and began to experiment with the wicked world of commercial art and graphic design. His family struggled financially and had given up a lot for his education, and the burden of wanting to earn was heavy.

Despite this, Paul's family was very supportive and he was able to continue a little longer. With his more commercially viable portfolio and a hint of sympathy for 'this local lad', he managed to enter the department of visual communications at the University of Wolverhampton, which covers graphic design and advertising. Not that it was yet clear, but Paul was on the verge of finding the career path he had been hunting for.

Bagging up oranges

'I was still dead set on becoming an illustrator', he remembers, 'or setting up a company doing window design. It wasn't until the last year that I surprised them by asking to look into advertising.' Wolverhampton did not see him as an ad-man, he was too quiet and they tried to discourage him. But he had a focus now and asked to be set advertising briefs. 'I think early on it was a sign that ad-men, ad directors, set their hands to most things. They have an appreciation of photography, typography, graphic design, illustration ... I didn't realise that at the time. But that was the early sign that I would do that.'

But as advertising began to unfold before Paul, money and its pressures still loomed in the background. His father was too ill to work and Paul was refused a grant to study under Thatcher's new scheme. Thus earning became a priority. He 'got a job on checkouts at Sainsbury's to make some money'. It is a sign of how far he has come that Paul now writes campaigns for Sainsbury's: 'try something new today' is a line straight from his pen. Just after this job, he was working on a market stall and starting to put advertising into practice. 'I wasn't bad at it. I worked out how you can polish up certain oranges and sell them for more money or how you could bag up the overripe. I was getting used to working out how to sell stuff.'

He even started to apply these techniques to his paintings, learning how to market, how to buy paint and the right brushes to add value, how to make a profit. He muses that 'my art and money always had this tension, which I think is why advertising was such an obvious choice. It's a way of using all your artistic skills, but essentially you're working out how to sell. Art and sales is actually advertising.'

He even started to apply market stall techniques to his paintings, learning how to market, how to buy paint and the right brushes to add value, how to make a profit.

The only ad agency in Birmingham

Verging ever closer to the world of advertising, Paul took a position within an illustration company but soon gave it up after he found it wasn't the job for him. He then found time to design and build a Santa's grotto at a local shopping centre. It was at this point, still seeking something elusive, that someone suggested he should speak to Cogents who 'did lots of exciting work with Rolls-Royce and were one of the biggest agencies outside of London'. With a 'don't ask, don't get' approach, he rang Cogents' office and was invited for a meeting. At the time he remembers thinking, 'God, this is easy' and is forthright in viewing it as a 'massive stroke of luck'. But luck still had one more gift to give.

Cogents was very positive about his portfolio and liked his work, but the company was confused by why he wanted to join it. By accident or chance, he was in the studio, where the ideas of art directors and copywriters are implemented, not the creative department upstairs, where he had wanted to be and wanted to work. Confident that this confident man had talent, someone from the studio took him up. 'So all of a sudden I had six creative directors looking at my portfolio.' Even now, the incredulity of being given such an impromptu interview can be heard in Paul's voice. Normally, something like this would be near impossible, but here he was. Confidence, insistence and luck had got him this far, but now it was down to talent and his portfolio.

The directors liked him and offered him a three-month work placement on the spot, a chance to learn the ropes. But the pressure of a career and money was constant and he was forced to refuse. A catalogue company had offered him a permanent job and he felt compelled to choose the security of this role. He couldn't afford to waste three months only to not be offered something, it did not matter that advertising might have been his calling. 'They were all very shocked. People were gathering around because they thought it was so entertaining that I was turning their placement down. Talk about naivety.' And there the story could have disappeared down another path, but Cogents was so impressed that one of the directors rang his mother and explained that they thought her son 'might have something, but she had to explain that the placement was necessary and no one just gets hired, that it was like an apprenticeship'.

Ever supportive, the director did just that. Paul began his placement and was subsequently hired. 'I was doing all the below the line stuff, scratch cards and basic ads and art direction, making tons and tons of mistakes and learning. It was very slow but I was learning and working with more senior writers all the time.' Cogents had proved to be so influential on Paul's career that his father never wanted him to leave. To him, this was now a job for life, but it would prove to be just the beginning. After two years he knew he had 'got it' and in the next two years he began to think about London, where he would need to move if he was to progress.

London

Paul wasn't able to afford frequent visits to the capital, neither time or money would allow it, so he took an unusual approach to advancing his career. As opposed to scheduling lots of interviews, he found one person in the industry who he trusted and 'decided to hang on to every word they said', a mentor. He met this mentor in his first London interview, where he was told that there was nothing in his portfolio that was usable. Paul remembers that 'gutted' feeling. It must have been similar to the injury that meant he couldn't trial at West Brom. 'I re-did my portfolio, all of it. I changed everything he said and when I went and saw him the second time he was really surprised because I had actually listened. It made him sit up and take me seriously.'

It took another revision before the portfolio was deemed worthy of the ad agencies of London. As tempting as it would have been to take his father's advice and stay with loyal Cogents, Paul continued to follow his ambition and improve his work. It is indicative of his character, even now his office is adorned with a poster that says 'perseverance furthers', which he claims as his motto. He conveys this message as if it is at the heart of everything he does, explaining that 'its amazing how if you just keep plugging away, if you don't lose enthusiasm, you can get somewhere' and it does seem to sum up a lot of Paul's story.

'I redid my portfolio, all of it. I changed everything he said and when I went and saw him the second time he was really surprised because I had actually listened. It made him sit up and take me seriously.'

After this third edit, he was told 'you've cracked this' and was put in touch with WCRS, a prominent marketing and advertising agency, who understandably loved the portfolio and hired him. He is one of the few Braziers to have left the Midlands and even now he looks back at the influence of his parents as essential in this move, giving him both the confidence and support to make it happen.

AMV and the present

London was always supposed to be temporary, perhaps a few years to help his career, but it is the place to be for the talented and ambitious. Paul was snapped up by AMV in 1991, after several years at WCRS working on

BMW and Carling Black Label, and it was here that Paul established him-self as one of Britain's best creatives in the advertising industry. He cer-tainly has the awards to prove it. It was also where he learnt the skills to make the step up to a position in management, which he did when he was made the Executive Creative Director (ECD) of AMV BBDO in 2005.

A highlight of Paul's career was his promotion to executive creative director at AMV, London's leading advertising agency.

'Becoming the ECD was me stepping into a management role, without any real training. Bizarrely in advertising you prove yourself by producing the best award-winning work, and by proving you can do this you get more and more senior. But along the way you have to learn how to manage people and you kind of do it on the job: handling creative and personal work, giving feedback.'

Paul continues to explain what management has taught him about advertising, and what advertising taught him about management. Seemingly, you do not reach this level in the industry with business degrees and management conferences, but with talent, appetite and creativity.

'It's a fascinating job. Psychology comes into it a lot. You have to understand who you are selling to and think what frame of mind people you are trying to convince to buy or donate are in. We are always trying to change people's behaviour. Psychology is also what you end up using a lot when you are running a department, you can't just lump them in as "creative people". Advertising is made up of introverts, extroverts, people who want to be in constant contact or like distance.'

Paul records this promotion as the biggest success of his career, bigger than his last of awards: six D&AD pencils, a dozen One Shows and top prize at Cannes as both a creative and Creative Director, and followed it up in 2010 by becoming president of D&AD, a British educational charity which promotes excellence in design and advertising. His work with

Paul was delighted to be selected as Chairman of the highly prestigious D&AD.

D&AD only hints at the passion he has for helping children and attempting to foster opportunity within the creative industries, especially for those let down by schools.

Looking back, it is with gratitude that he remembers his success and he is humble when he says 'I never thought I would have the chance to be in this position and work with some of the country's most talented and creative people, it's such a fantastic thing.'

Today and tomorrow

Listening to Paul talk about his work, hearing the genuine enjoyment and passion in his voice, is almost enough to make one seek out advertising recruitment boards and start work on a portfolio. Although it is obvious that he is well suited to the intensity of the work. 'I'm obsessed with my work, it drives me mad as well, it's an obsession, I have the compulsive desire to solve briefs, I just can't leave them alone. As soon as I know there is a problem in the building it drives me crazy, I have to solve it.'

But this is quickly tempered by the enviable claims that 'I don't have a desk, we come in here and sit on sofas and kick around ideas. I like it like this, casual and relaxed. It is a very creative environment.' And it is creativity that underpins his work, even when having to manage 38 teams and 60 separate creatives. While allocating briefs and helping his teams reach their goals, it is perhaps unsurprising that he still finds the time and enthusiasm to write his own campaigns.

'We are the biggest ad agency in the country and one of the most creative in the world, that's on record with awards, and I have helped build one of the best creative departments and I am so proud of it. I guess the future is just about keeping that together and improving it. We'd never be complacent. And I am so interested in working with young people and encouraging them and promoting Britain as "the creative island". I am passionate about this. And I have had to leave my footballing ambitions behind.'

His advice for anyone looking to become part of the industry is to 'pick a mentor whose work you respect. See your mentor three times, developing your book significantly after each time. Listen to every word. Go with their advice. Don't resist.' He is sure to leave with 'perseverance furthers' ringing in your head.

CRITIC

Mark Kermode

Current title: film critic

Age and DOB: 49 (b. 1963)

First job: paper round

Other careers: presenter, musician (plays the double bass and harmonica in skiffle band The Dodge Brothers)

Most well known for: his BBC film reviews and blog

Being shot at with Werner Herzog and hand-bagged by Dame Helen Mirren are not tales one would expect to hear from someone whose job description is, essentially, to watch and review films. Yet, Mark Kermode is not the average film critic: he has been voted as the most trusted British film critic in a recent YouGov poll and came 75th in *The Guardian*'s list of powerful people in the world of film. While Mark claims that his reviews carry no weight with box office figures, his passionate reviews and comments on all things film are viewed, listened to and read by hundreds of thousands of people every week. His Radio 5 Live show alone gets 540,000 regular listeners and 250,000 downloads each week. This has given Mark a solid platform from which to preach his unapologetically controversial views, such as *High School Musical 3* being one of the best films of 2008, and that *Sex and the City 2* is 'vomit inducing'. These opinions are especially unexpected from someone who cut his teeth on writing reviews of horror films, and who claims that *The Exorcist* is the 'greatest film ever made'.

His honest and often surprising set of opinions, which Mark presents with an uncontrolled passion, are not only among the keys to his enduring popularity, but also something that helped him get to where he is today.

Early life

Born in Barnet in 1963, Mark claims that 'if you were a kid in the seventies, things could seem pretty grim what with power cuts and three day weeks'. The cinema soon became his escape, taking him to 'the circus, different countries and even the moon'. Mark soon developed an almost monomanic obsession for film. 'I didn't do sport, I didn't go to parties with, you know, friends and that sort of thing. I went to the pictures.' He even began to develop his love of horror films at home, sneaking out of bed to watch *The Monday X Film* on television. This love of films made him realise very early on that he wanted a career that would involve being in the cinema as much as possible, 'even if it was working as an usher or in the projection room'.

However, while film was Mark's major love as a teenager, he was also passionate about music, being a huge fan of the *New Musical Express* (NME) while at school. A 'schoolboyish' satirical letter that Mark sent the magazine, which was a dramatisation of an imaginary and flamboyant discussion between two NME writers, was the first time he saw his own writing in print. This early love of writing made him begin to consider criticism as his preferred route for a life in the cinema, and resulted in many scrappy film reviews that he kept in a notebook, intended for reading by no one but himself. Mark's writing abilities served him well in school, doing well in English, or, as Mark puts it, doing 'less badly in English than anything else'.

Mark left school with average grades and was initially 'rejected from every university that I applied to, even the one my school said didn't reject anybody'. However, Mark was determined not only to go to university, but to go to university in Manchester, which he understood 'had not only an exciting music scene, but also a thriving journalist scene with many of the NME writers based there'. Mark decided to take a year out, where he worked in 'the stationery department of a London hospital' before re-applying. This time he was accepted.

Manchester educated

On arriving in Manchester, Mark claims that he quickly mutated 'from snot-nosed NME-reading angsty teenager to a red-flag-waving bolshie bore', but his love of film and desire to become a film critic remained unchanged. Becoming one, however, wasn't so easy. Mark found the biggest difficulty with breaking in to film criticism was a problem that still plagues budding film critics today: how do you get into preview screenings? Mark describes this as catch-22. 'You can't get into the preview screening because you aren't published, and you can't publish a film review because you can't get into a preview.' The only thing he claims you can do to break the cycle is, if you can't find anyone willing to send you, 'just turn up and hope somebody else lets you in.' Initially, this 'try your luck' approach wasn't particularly successful for Mark so he turned his hand to writing gig reviews for the student newspaper *Mancunion*, which he claimed would 'publish pretty much anything'.

Eventually, Mark managed to get a part-time job selling advertising space for the small, but growing, magazine *City Life*. Here, Mark was given two frequent jobs: selling advertising space, in which he only succeeded in 'losing money hand over fist', and driving the *City Life* van, which he promptly crashed. However, these two spectacular failures, which most would expect would have led to his sacking, actually managed to get Mark exactly what he wanted – a writing role. It was deemed safest to stick him behind a desk. It was here that his special interest in horror fiction and film that he had clung on to since childhood paid off. *City Life* needed a review of *The Return of the Living Dead* and Mark was the only one who had seen it. After he had written 'a very nerdy horror-fan film review', the film editors realised that he was a horror expert and began sending him to previews. This gave Mark the belief that he maintains to this day: that being authoritative in one area is 'very important. It gives you a way in'.

Mark's fascination with all things horror was also serving him well academically, and, after finishing his degree, he decided to undertake his PhD on 'the radical, ethical and political implications of modern British and American horror fiction'. Mark says that this period of postgraduate study was 'really valuable because I loved reading and I loved writing and I wanted to get better at it', which he did, because Mark claims his mentor (and former tutor) Arnold Hinchcliffe 'taught me how to write'. As well as this, balancing the PhD with his journalism through 'being rigid about doing four and a half hours of the PhD every day before doing the journalism' taught Mark to manage his time and work to deadlines. However, while all of these elements made a huge impact on the future of Mark's career, arguably the most important thing to emerge from his decision to stay studying at Manchester was that he met his future wife 'and harshest critic'.

They first met when Mark was required to read a chapter of his thesis to a group of university tutors and fellow students, which Linda attended. Afterwards, Linda spoke to Mark and the first thing she said to him was, 'I think your thesis is haunted by Freud', which Mark maintains 'is one of the greatest opening lines to a relationship ever'. It was love at first sight for Mark, and he applied the same dedication to Linda that he did to his writing, spending 'the next few years wearing her down to make her realise that it was love at first sight for her also'. Mark maintains that her 'much more organised mind' has kept her firmly as his most stringent editor, and that everything he has written since has been 'heavily subbed by Linda'. However, even with some experience at *City Life* and a PhD, Mark soon realised that it took more than a good CV to get a full-time job as a critic.

The front

By 1991 Mark had finally handed in his PhD thesis and worn Linda down to a point where she agreed to marry him. They took their honeymoon in America, where Mark was determined to see the setting of *The Exorcist* in Georgetown. To mark the event, one his former colleagues at *City Life* ran an article in the *Manchester Evening News* entitled 'Dr Horror plans haunted honeymoon'. Meanwhile, Mark had set about attempting to find full-time work in London.

Having moved to London in 1988, Mark immediately began touring the offices of various magazines and handing in photocopies of his reviews, but without any success. Eventually, he entered the offices of *Time Out*, where he asked the receptionist to speak to the magazine's film editors Brian Case or Geoff Andrew, who Mark explained he knew. After finally managing to meet them, Mark proceeded to claim that he had spoken to both men previously when working at *City Life* and that they had told him that if he was ever in London they would give him a job. Confused and bemused, it soon emerged that Mark had experience doing listings and that they required someone to fill that position there with the weak possibility of being given the occasional piece of writing. Mark maintains, in a typically self-deprecating manner, that this approach to getting hired was the sole key to his success in this period. 'I wasn't blessed with much talent or intelligence, but I had a lot of front.'

After spending a few months being 'really terrible at listings at *Time Out*, Mark decided that he could not carry on in good conscience and went to Geoff to offer his resignation, acknowledging that he was letting the magazine down. This was, of course, something that Geoff had realised and he admitted to Mark that, if it hadn't been for his honesty, he would have had to sack him. However, Mark's clear commitment to doing a good job for the magazine turned another disastrous situation into a golden opportunity as Geoff offered Mark his first drip-feed of minor film reviews while keeping him employed to answer phones and do basic admin around the offices.

While the writing of this period was only minor, having Geoff as his editor was a formative time in Mark's career, and quickly made him realise that the best experience for any film critic is 'being edited by someone who knows more than you do'. Shaping Mark's writing and giving him print space in a magazine weren't the only opportunities Mark found at *Time Out*, instead, the largest benefit of his time there was that it opened his door into the world of radio. This was a door that Mark, again, managed to pass through thanks to his amazing levels of front, or as Mark also calls it 'the confidence of complete stupidity'.

On one normal day at *Time Out*, Mark was answering the phones when he got a call from someone asking for one of their writers who knew about film to do some video reviews on LBC radio. While the writer they wanted was away for two weeks, Mark immediately volunteered to fill his space until then, claiming that he had 'loads' of radio experience.

When broadcasting day arrived, Mark turned up to the radio station expecting a comfortable and relaxed briefing before the broadcast, but was immediately led upstairs, plonked in a chair and asked for his opinion on the week's films. Mark remembers panicking and losing control of his voice, babbling on about anything and everything. As soon as it was over Mark felt awful, knowing that he had spoken undecipherable gibberish to the city of London. Despite this, he was surprised to be asked back the next week. This time he prepared a script in advance, learnt it off by heart and delivered it perfectly on air. When he left the booth, the programme editor asked him what was wrong, claiming that 'we preferred it last week, you know, when you pretended you didn't know what you were doing?' Whilst this spell on radio was only temporary at LBC, it was key in getting him into the BBC, where Mark really made his name.

Mark is now a household name in the world of film.

At the BBC

In the few years after his brief radio stint, Mark managed to get writing spots in various magazines such as *Fangoria, Vox* and the NME and was slowly getting more recognition for his film criticism. Mark claims that, at each of these places, 'I was really lucky to be taken under the wing of a very good editor who bashed my copy into shape.'

One day, out of the blue, Mark got a phone call from the presenter he had briefly worked with at LBC, Sarah Ward. She asked if he would come on as a regular film critic for BBC Radio 5. Mark agreed, and it was here that he worked with Danny Baker, an experience which Mark describes as 'like walking on the deck of a ship in the middle of a storm' but from whom he learnt 'major lessons in broadcasting': mainly, think on your feet and don't change your opinions for anybody. From here, Mark moved to Radio 1, where he worked with Mark Radcliffe, Mary Anne-Hobbs and his future broadcasting partner Simon Mayo.

In his radio experience, Mark believes that a key to his success was that he had a growing experience of writing, noting that the: 'the best critics on the radio (of which I do not count myself) have written, it's an important part of the discipline because you learn how to construct an argument.' However, Mark believes that just as his writing benefited from a strong editor, so his radio career has been helped by working with a succession of excellent broadcasters. This is, Mark maintains, one of the main reasons why he has worked for so long with Simon Mayo. Their broadcasting partnership has existed at Radio 5 Live since 2001 and seen them win numerous broadcasting awards, the success of which Mark puts down solely to Simon. 'Simon is the best broadcaster in the country because he makes everyone in the country think that he's talking to them, this enables me to talk to him and he can talk to them.'

'The best critics on the radio (of which I do not count myself) have written, it's an important part of the discipline because you learn how to construct an argument.'

The success of Mark's radio career twinned with his writing career has led him into other areas with the BBC, most notably as a presenter on *The Culture Show* as well as running his extremely popular BBC video blog 'Kermode Uncut', which has extended his critical opinions far beyond the British Isles and has made him a firm favourite with the internet generation.

Mark keeps his writing skills from rusting through his various books and his weekly 'DVD roundup' for *The Observer*, which he loves because 'it gives me 1,000 words to go "and another thing"'. Mark has also written four books: *It's Only a Movie, The Good the Bad and the Multiplex*, and two British Film Institute 'Modern Classics' volumes on *The Exorcist* and *The Shawshank Redemption*, all of which have given him the opportunity to offer and support 'an extended argument'.

Ambitions and advice

Mark is very aware of this enviable position. 'There are film critics who are much better than me but who are thirsting for work because the market for film critics has dried up.' Why is this? Mark muses, 'People have got this idea that film critics have a rarefied snobby view of the world, which is baloney.' In fact, Mark claims that any budding film critic must take care to swim against this popular opinion by reading the work of critics who are already out there. 'I'm not saying that there's value in what I do, but if you don't think it's worth listening to critics such as Nigel Floyd, Anne Billson, Alan Jones or Kim Newman then you don't know what you're talking about.'

Beyond requiring a passion for film and the need to appreciate the writing of other critics, Mark admits that things have changed a great deal since he broke into criticism, and that, while he could turn up and demand a job, 'nowadays you wouldn't get through the front door like that … it's locked down a lot more today, now you have to have what's called a unique selling point'. While he sees blogging as a potential entry point for today's critics, he's sceptical about this route because it doesn't give writers the chance to be edited, saying: 'writing what you want isn't always the best thing, you need a second pair of eyes'.

'If you don't think it's worth listening to critics such as Nigel Floyd, Anne Bilson, Alan Jones or Kim Newman, then you don't know what you're talking about.'

However, Mark says it can be done, but that you need a strong work ethic and a realisation that 'there's no short-cut for doing your homework.' The need to work hard clearly doesn't go away with increased experience, fame and popularity, as can be seen by Mark's typical working week:

'Mondays and Tuesdays are viewing screenings, writing on the train for an hour and a half each way. I write my books, do research for the blog, and film for *The Culture Show* and other projects on Wednesday and Thursday before broadcasting on Friday. I start early in the morning and end late at night.' Behind his madcap tales of celebrity run-ins and reputation for being a motor-mouthed film geek, it's clear that he invests a lot of hard work in everything that he does. But, he's doing what he loves, and when asked where he'd like to take his criticism in the future, he simply responds: 'to be honest, if I can continue doing these things until I drop off my perch then that would be great.'

DJ

Andi Durrant

Current title: DJ

Age and DOB: 31 (b. 1981)

First job: tech op

Other careers: owned a small record company, named Nubreed, created club night label named Elektrik Playground, created a new music-selling website GoSound, due to launch Winter 2012/2013

Most well known for: presenting on Capital FM

Aged 31, Andi Durrant is grateful that he leads a 'charmed and lucky life'. As one half of Riley and Durrant, the Capital FM DJ has performed in every continent and currently gets paid to fly to Mallorca and Ibiza every week to entertain crowds of thousands. However, Andi did not get to where he is today through good fortune alone, having struggled to the top of his field through hard work, sacrifice and at times pure brazenness. While not all of his business ventures have been a success, Andi's unwavering determination and his ability to learn from mistakes has aided his career: 'if you want to be in this industry you have to understand that you won't get an opportunity handed to you. You have to go out there and make it happen.'

Seizing an opportunity

Andi's interest in music came early and he began piano lessons at the age of eight. However he soon grew bored of this childhood hobby and by the time he was 13, Andi had quit piano lessons in favour of playing computer games and hanging out with his school friends. Yet just a few years later, while on a German exchange trip, Andi managed to sneak into a nightclub, despite being only 15 years old, where he discovered a new genre of music that completely captivated him: 'It caught my ear and really excited me. I became mad for electronic and dance music.' On returning home to the small Yorkshire town of Mirfield, Andi immediately set about buying as many CDs as he could and when a new radio station named Kiss 105 started up in Leeds, he was immediately drawn to it: 'It totally blew my mind. It was music I had never heard before. It was like something out of this world.' Awe-struck, Andi immediately wrote to the producers and asked if he could come to the studio to participate in some work experience, but the letter was ignored. However, Andi was not about to give up on his dream that easily and four letters later, he eventually received a phone call, asking him to come into the studio for a chat.

Once there Andi admitted that at age 16, he had no prior experience, but after promising to be a fast learner, he managed to persuade the programme controller to allow him to come every Sunday and do 'general dogsbody work'. Andi showed his dedication to the role for four months and by the time he started sixth form college at the age of 17, he was given his first paid job in radio as a tech op. This involved travelling to Leeds straight from school and spending every Friday and Saturday night playing out shows that had been pre-recorded by the radio station's presenters, for which he received £50 a weekend. Yet, while the job meant sacrificing going out with his friends and the sleepless nights made studying difficult, Andi felt honoured to 'actually be able to touch things' in the radio station and he remained in the position for a year.

While working as a tech op, Andi made full use of the equipment and took the opportunity to make presenting demos, which he gave to his bosses, asking them to critique his work. Despite his early demos being 'awful', Andi was not deterred and after copying the work of other presenters, he eventually developed his own style. On New Year's Day 1998, Andi was asked to step in for a presenter who was on holiday and present his very own radio show. From then on, he began to cover increasingly more shows when presenters were away or ill and through showing a willingness to jump in at the last minute, he earned a reputation for being reliable. In the same year, Kiss 105 became Galaxy and many staff were made redundant. However, as a 'nobody', Andi managed to slip under the radar and remain at the station after the change-over.

With the transformation to Galaxy, the radio station began to host club nights around Yorkshire and Andi was asked to DJ at some of the big commercial clubs in the area. The following year, at just 18, his career prospects soared even further, when he was offered his own show on air every Friday night. However, with more responsibility came more sacrifices and in the same year, Andi was forced to decide whether or not he was going to attend university, which was what his parents had hoped for. Eventually, Andi came to the conclusion to skip university and focus on his radio show, telling his parents, 'If I don't do this now, I never will.' Luckily, Andi's parents were extremely supportive of his decision, but he sees similar dilemmas played out for radio interns time and time again: 'I can see who has the drive to make it and who doesn't.'

For some, the decision comes after university and it is a choice between staying in a fairly well-paid job, or throwing caution to the wind and following their dream of working in radio. Either way, Andi explains that eventually a gamble has to be made, as setting up a career in radio requires 100% focus: 'The worst thing that can happen is that you'll be skint for two years and you will have to rely on support from the people around you. But if you're willing to learn and you truly believe that you can do it, then I honestly think that anyone can make it.'

For some, it is a choice between staying in a fairly well-paid job, or throwing caution to the wind and following their dream of working in radio.

Persistence is key

Alongside hosting club nights, in 2002 Galaxy Radio began to fly DJs out to Ibiza and host a week of live broadcasts from the Spanish Island. However, as a young inexperienced DJ of 21, Andi was left behind. Yet, relentless as ever, Andi decided to take matters into his own hands, funding his own air fare and accommodation and travelling to Ibiza at the same time as his colleagues: 'I was a complete pest and said, "Look, I've got all my records with me, shall I just record my show in Ibiza while I'm here?"' The self-subsidised trip paid off and the following year Galaxy paid Andi to record his show in Ibiza. In the meantime, Andi had grown tired of his club nights in the UK, where he simply played other people's music, as he was 'into the more weird and wonderful side of music' and enjoyed mixing sounds.

After going to a nightclub named Gatecrasher in Sheffield, which he remembers as 'the clubbing Mecca of the North of England,' Andi instantly knew what his next goal would be: 'I stood in the crowd looking up at the DJ and thought, "Wow, that is where I want to be. I want to see how I command thousands of people"'. Andi began producing his own music and handing mix-tapes to the staff at Gatecrasher, who were at first dismissive. However, once again he showed persistence: 'I started harassing people and doing demo tapes and if the mix wasn't right I'd just

Andi secured a gig DJing in Ibiza through sheer persistence.

have to do it again and again until they eventually just said, '"Yes ok, you can have half an hour at the start".'

It was while working his first night at Gatecrasher in 2002 that Andi met his future business partner and fellow DJ, Nick Riley. Yet Andi was met with a cold greeting from Nick at first, who had similarly just persuaded the bosses at the nightclub to give him a shot: 'I could see him thinking, "Who are you and why are you muscling in on my job?"' Determined to ease the tension between his new co-worker and himself, Andi invited Nick onto his Friday night show, where they soon hit it off.

Discovering that he worked well with Nick, Andi asked him to the make-shift studio in the rented bedroom of his new flat in Leeds and they soon started to produce tracks of trance music together. Although their early attempts were ignored by record labels, to whom the tracks were sent, by the following year the DJ duo had finally produced something worth listening to and their track 'Candesco' was signed by a small, independent record label named Recover Records. While only 500 vinyls were produced, Andi felt a huge sense of achievement: 'To hold in your hand a real track that we had made was the most amazing feeling in the world.'

Andi and Nick were pleased to sell just 300 of the original vinyls but it was not until they handed the track to Dutch DJ, Tiesto, that things really started to get exciting for the pair. Today, Tiesto is one of the most famous DJs in the world, but back in 2003, he was just beginning to build his name and so on meeting him through work at Gatecrasher, Andi and Nick seized the opportunity to introduce him to their music.

On 10 May 2003, Tiesto introduced an entirely new concept to the DJ scene and became the first DJ to host a solo concert in a stadium, in the Dutch football ground GelreDome. During this event, Tiesto played 'Candesco' to the crowd of 25,000 people, with whom it was a huge hit. With the release of the concert DVD, 'Candesco' received even more attention and soon other artists began to ask if they could mix their tracks with Andi and Nick's song. Building up their brand name as 'Riley and Durrant', Andi and Nick released more trance music under Tiesto's own record label, Black Hole and other European record labels, such as United. Moreover, the 500 original copies of 'Candesco', released by Recover Records, went on to become a collectors' item, selling for around £50 each on eBay.

Soon other artists began to ask if they could mix their tracks with Andi and Nick's song.

Andi performing as one half of Riley and Durrant.

Getting serious

In the meantime, in 2003, Andi had managed to seal his first Ibiza club performance. While in Ibiza first time around in 2002, he experienced Cream at Amnesia, one of the biggest Ibiza club nights of the time and once again used his powers of persuasion to get himself a gig, offering to DJ in the club for the following 2003 season for free: 'I was able to play in the club that I'd always wanted to play in through blagging my way in and I smashed it, so the following year they paid me.'

With the success of 'Candesco' under their belt, soon Nick and Andi began to perform at increasingly impressive club scenes as a duo, and were promoted to the prime slot at Gatecrasher. Moreover, they began to tour all around the world and alongside regular slots in Ibiza, in 2004 they became one of a few British acts to play at Fort Dance Festival at St Petersburg.

Nonetheless, in 2004 the pair were still not 'big enough' to be signed by a DJ agency, which would set up their gigs for them and so in an act of resourcefulness, they decided to create one of their own. By night the business partners would produce their own trance tracks in their rented studio in Leeds and by day they would use the office space to set up gigs and radio shows for other rising DJs. However, despite maintaining the business for a couple of years and making money for many DJs, Andi and Nick made a loss on their investments, funding all the costs on multiple credit cards and receiving little return on the agency set-ups.

Nonetheless, the duo profited greatly in experience: 'The only reason we set up a proper company and got an office was because we felt that this was how you got successful but it wasn't. You don't really need any of that fancy stuff. The whole experience was a massive learning curve.' Consequently, Andi and Nick dropped the DJ agency and moved to a small studio in the centre of Leeds to concentrate on producing their own tracks.

The tracks continued to sell well, and the duo had created an effective formula in which they knew the sound and the format they were using in each track and were able to create a new track or remix every day. However, Andi and Nick were not content to take the easy road and so in 2006 they decided to change styles, moving away from the trance scene and into a far bigger mix of genres, including house, electro and even folk: 'We'd become almost bored of it. I guess when anything gets too easy you need a change.'

Research and development

After spending most of 2006 working to create an entirely new sound, Andi released his debut album, 'Research and Development', with Nick in 2007. Having produced numerous remixes in previous years for Tim Binns of Newstate Music, Andi and Nick had built a strong friendship with the talent scout. Consequently, their new album was signed by Newstate Music before it had even been produced and Tim mentored them through the process. The album reached the iTunes top 50 in the first month of sales and received excellent critical acclaim for its unique blend of genres.

Moreover, experimenting with a variety of music styles proved beneficial to his radio career and Andi was offered a prime slot at Galaxy on Saturdays from 5pm to 7pm, in addition to his Friday night show. Proof of the new show's success came in 2007 when Andi was nominated for a Sony Academy Music Award: 'For someone who had just grown up in a small Yorkshire town and never even met anyone famous, it was a really big deal.' Andi was soon to feel even more awestruck on receiving the Bronze Award for Music Broadcaster of the Year.

The album reached the iTunes top 50 in the first month of sales and received excellent critical acclaim for its unique blend of genres.

Entrepreneurial spirit

Ever-determined to challenge themselves, in 2007 Andi and Nick formed their own record label, named Nu Breed, with the aim of signing the new tracks that Andi was regularly sent to play on his Friday night show. Yet the following year, after gaining knowledge of the music industry and rising above the title of newly formed artists themselves, Andi and Nick dropped the label to continue on their journey to success: 'We had got what we needed out of it and it was time to focus on what was next.'

Using the contacts that they had made though their previous business ventures, in 2008 Andi and Nick combined with DJ Adam Sherridan and club promoter Nick Ferguson to form Electrik Playground, a monthly event in Leeds' biggest clubs. Following success in Leeds, the group managed to land a huge weekly gig in Ibiza for the 2008 and 2009 summer season. Flying out to Ibiza every Friday, before performing to crowds of 10,000 people in Privilege, the biggest club in the world, the business served to build up the name of everyone involved. In 2009 Electrik Playground branched into a record label and the company produced and released a

Andi has always created his own opportunities, starting numerous business ventures alongside his DJing.

number of successful tracks. By 2010, the company had stopped working together, but once again Andi had enjoyed an amazing experience and built upon his ever-expanding contact list.

Going for gold

Andi's radio show was continuing to impress his fans and in 2009 he improved on his previous success, winning the Sony Gold Award for Music Broadcaster of the Year, followed by the Sony Silver Award for Best Specialist Music Programme in 2010. Andi's success caught the attention of Radio 1 bosses in 2009 and he received a provisional offer to work for the national radio station: 'It had always been my aim to work for Radio 1, ever since I was a kid starting out on radio.' However his hopes were suddenly shattered when the results of a BBC trust review revealed that Radio 1 needed to focus on a younger audience: 'I was told that at 28, I was too old. It was a massive blow to be told my dream wouldn't come true.'

Andi had even more reason to fear for the future of his radio career when in 2010, the owners of Global Radio bought out many radio stations and Galaxy became part of Capital FM. At the same time, Andi encouraged his producer to take a new job with Kiss FM and while this was a positive career move for his colleague, it left Andi without a producer in a radio station that was about to make many DJs redundant.

However, by this time, Andi had a lot of experience in pushing for what he wanted and so he got in touch with the chief executive officer of Global Radio and managed to persuade them that the new Capital FM should experiment with specialist music: 'It was like being 17 again. I had to fight for my own job.' In the last few years, Nick had occasionally come into the studio to co-present Andi's evening shows and after further discussion with the Capital FM bosses, they came to an arrangement in which Nick would produce Andi's radio shows, broadcast between 11pm and 1am every Friday and Saturday. Fortunately, this alternative path turned out for the better and in a review in 2012, Andi's radio shows had overtaken Radio 1 in the national ratings.

It takes two

Throughout Andi's career, his radio show and his work as 'Riley and Durrant' had always been kept as two separate entities, however with

Nick working full time at the radio station, the two began to merge and the pair decided to rebrand 'Riley and Durrant' and focus solely on 'Andi Durrant'. While Andi is now the face of the business, the duo continue to perform their club events together, sharing all profits evenly. While Andi's strengths lie in the creativity of producing music, Nick has a business mind and Andi believes that working together has been the 'only reason' for their success: 'It's better to halve your income from the start and have a partner that enables you to do twice the work – it'll always end up making you more successful in the long run.' Under the new title of 'Andi Durrant' the pair have been asked by the organisers of club events Mallorca and Ibiza Live to host a weekly gig on each island respectively, performing with the likes of Tinie Tempah, Rizzle Kicks, JLS and Jessie J.

Such an amazing opportunity involves a great deal of travel and following a fully funded flight to Mallorca every Sunday, Andi holds a gig at BCM Planet Dance that evening. He then hosts an afternoon gig in Mallorca every Tuesday, before getting flown out to Ibiza to perform the same night. However, there is no time for relaxation for Andi in Ibiza, as he flies back to the UK on Wednesday mornings, to spend time with his two young sons and wife, Liz, before heading to the radio studio on Thursdays to prepare for the weekend show, which takes place on Friday and Saturday night.

'It's better to halve your income from the start and have a partner that enables you to do twice the work – it'll always end up making you more successful in the long run.'

During his hectic week, Andi finds time to produce music with Nick in the studio space that is lent to them by Capital FM, before flying back to Mallorca on Sundays. Despite the chaotic nature of his week for the Ibiza season between June and September, Andi would not swap his jet-setting lifestyle for any typical nine to five: 'I wake up every morning and look forward to going to work. I don't think many people can say that.'

Moreover, Andi and business partner Nick have continued to experiment with innovative new business concepts and he believes that their latest venture, which combines all of the knowledge and contacts obtained through their previous endeavours, may just be the one to watch. Gosound is Andi and Nick's new company, which aims to completely change the way that people buy and sell music downloads. While most artists despair at the detrimental effect of illegal music

Andi and Nick still perform together but have rebranded as just 'Andi Durrant'.

downloads on the music industry, Andi and Nick have viewed this as an opportunity to create a worldwide business solution. Consequently, when he is not hopping on and off aircraft, Andi is currently trying to make the life-changing decision of whether or not to involve an external investor in his new business.

For Andi, simply gliding through an occupation has never been an option and after spending his entire career experimenting with new ways to challenge himself, he unsurprisingly states 'taking the road less travelled' as a key requirement in his field of work. Andi fought for his high-profile work experience at the age of 16 and through determination alone, he has managed to stay with the same radio station through two disruptive changeovers that could have easily cost him his job: 'Just getting your foot in the door is the biggest milestone – if you do that and you're driven, and you really want it, that's all you need. If you don't have the drive then the opportunity will be wasted.'

As for producing music, Andi highlights individuality as the secret to success. Receiving over 800 tapes a week from hopeful artists, Andi has heard his fair share of unimaginative copies of famous hits. 'If you really want to be an artist,' he says, 'you have to try and be different.' While some of Andi's business ventures have been more successful than others, Andi believes 'it is important to make lots of mistakes so you can learn how to do it properly when you're a grownup.' With the important Gosound business decision looming over his head, Andi suddenly feels that he has indeed finally matured, however, the 31-year-old is not willing to let his night-clubbing career die any time soon: 'I'm sure everyone must reach the point where they think that this is a young person's game, but I certainly haven't. I'll still be going for at least the next 10 years.'

FASHION MAGAZINE EDITOR-IN-CHIEF

Trish Halpin

Current title: editor-in-chief

Age: 45

First job: hole-puncher in a Filofax factory

Other careers: always worked in publishing

Most well known for: her work on *Marie Claire*

Even in a mad morning rush, Trish Halpin makes time to look stunning. It's her job. Before work she mulls over what to wear, pairing her outfit with just the right handbag and killer heels. 'I have this wardrobe of amazing clothes where I think if this job stopped tomorrow, what would I do with all these clothes as I wouldn't be able to wear them anywhere else!'

As editor-in-chief of *Marie Claire*, Trish is the brand ambassador of the thinking woman's glossy, keen to deliver compelling articles and photoshoots on fashion and beauty to the magazine's 250,000 readers. Her clothes are an extension of what the magazine represents, and while the pressure is on, Trish finds getting dressed for work empowering.

Behind the attire is a twice winner of the Editor of the Year Award with 20 years' experience in editorial. However, she's still human. 'If people saw what I wear on the weekend, they would never think I'm the editor of a fashion magazine!'

Tour de force

Raised with a strong work ethic, Trish has had at least a part-time job since she was 16. During her summer holidays at university she had a job in a factory, punching holes into the leather casings of Filofaxes all day. Unsurprisingly, this didn't suit as a lifelong career, and when she graduated from Brighton Polytechnic with a degree in English and media studies, she took any admin work she could get her hands on. A friend had started working in the Department for Transport and told her a job had come up doing the production for the classified advertising. She went along for an interview (which had decidedly not been scheduled into a Filofax) and got the role.

Publishing wasn't something Trish had ever thought she could do. 'During my education at a state comprehensive Catholic school, you weren't pushed or inspired to think you could do something amazing. It was always working in a bank or as a secretary – not that there's anything wrong with those jobs – but that was it, even if you had a degree. I think that's changed a lot for young people, in particular young women, today. You can achieve the role that you want and work in a creative industry.'

With her school lacking in imagination and her family not connected to publishing, Trish found support elsewhere. She met her future husband at university and his career began to parallel hers. As the Mr and Mrs of magazines, he did photography while she did production. 'It became our world. He knew the people I was working with, because as you move around magazines, you tend to keep seeing the same people. We were in it together. It's always been useful to have someone who understands what's involved.'

A lifelong lover of magazines, she remembers the launch of *Marie Claire*: 'It was fresh, exciting and different from any other women's magazine out there'. Glenda Bailey OBE, current editor-in-chief of *Harper's Bazaar*, had been the brains behind the launch and inspired Trish to reach what she saw as the pinnacle of magazine editing. 'She'd done a documentary called *Absolutely Marie Claire* and at the time it was something everyone was talking about. She was a bit of a legend. I thought being the editor of *Marie Claire* must be the best job in the business, because of the strength in the features and fashion balance.'

From then on, working for *Marie Claire* became a lifelong dream and Trish got as much experience as she could to reach her goal. From classified advertising, she moved to a newspaper called *Screen International* as a layout sub-editor. This job involved working with the copy to amend any errors, factual or grammatical, and make it fit the newspaper's style and target audience. Sub-editors also lay out the text, design the pages, do picture research and solve issues such as too much or not enough content. Trish advises those looking to go into publishing that they shouldn't start too narrow and risk not getting in at all. 'I worked in business-to-business newspapers and contract publishing. That's something you shouldn't overlook. People who want to get into publishing might start out thinking "I've got to work on a glossy, I want to aim high". It's great to have that ambition, but to think you're going to start there is unrealistic due to how competitive it is.'

Trish advises those looking to go into publishing that they shouldn't start too narrow and risk not getting in at all.

Her detailed work in a fast-paced environment at *Screen International* showed she had the skills needed for magazine editing. *More!* was her first taste of women's consumer magazines, then *New Woman*. Here she was involved in the shopping fashion pages, but her eye was always on the prize of women's glossies. Her broad background coupled with the amount of experience showed genuine interest and dedication to the publishing industry, and put her CV on the top of the pile when she applied for the deputy editor position at *Red*. 'It was a huge leap, because it's not the normal route to become an editor. It took my career in a different direction.'

While people have an expectation of one star-studded party after another in magazine publishing, it was many nights of hard graft in the office to meet deadlines which helped Trish climb the ladder to the top. After surviving the chasm from production to editorial, she reached the summit when she achieved her first editorship: the editor of *Red* went on maternity leave and she became the acting editor. 'I'd always thought I couldn't do it, I wasn't grand enough. I was the person behind the scenes putting it all together. When I was acting editor, I realised I can do this. There was obviously a lack of confidence, even though I was doing what the role required. It was a lightbulb moment.'

The many nights of hard graft in the office to meet deadlines helped Trish climb the ladder to the top.

While at *Red*, Trish won Editor of the Year not once, but twice. The award is run by the British Society of Magazine Editors, judged by editors and external media experts. 'To be voted for by your peers essentially is a fantastic achievement.' Trish attributes her second win to competing against another magazine which poached some of her staff and launched into the same arena as *Red*. She upped her game and increased the magazine's sales dramatically. 'Keeping an eye on your competitors is so important, making sure you're watching what they're doing and out-doing them.'

In 2006 she was approached with the job offer of editor of *InStyle*. Persuaded, Trish joined the magazine, which calls itself 'your personal shopper and friend to the stars' as it celebrated its fifth birthday. A party is serious business in fashion, and *InStyle's* red carpet event was no exception. Fifteen designer gowns were exhibited at the Victoria and Albert Museum, including Elizabeth Hurley's 'safety pin' dress and Kate Winslet's red silk Ben de Lisi. Invitation-only, naturally.

Both *InStyle* and *Marie Claire* are owned by ICP Media and in 2009 her boss asked if she wanted to move to *Marie Claire*. 'What else could I say, it was my dream job.'

Avant-garde

With a strapline of 'Think smart, look amazing', *Marie Claire* aims to reflect the modern, educated woman: a balance of intelligent, eye-opening features combined with a strong beauty aesthetic. As an international brand, 'to have that world view and to represent women around the world is unique to *Marie Claire* still'.

The combination of the recession with huge changes in the media landscape, such as free media and the move to digital, has brought its own challenges for *Marie Claire*. 'Budgets are cut, roles are cut, and then you're told to make the magazine more. At the time it's not very pleasant, but then you do it and achieve it, and you come out better at the other end.'

This promise to be more than paper and ink (or, increasingly, pixels), means Trish's calendar is so busy she has a personal assistant to help her keep track of every meeting, event and deadline thrown at her. Her Mondays are focused on planning and start with a production update meeting. She sits with the editorial team to review where they are with that month's issue, including what copy and pictures are outstanding, and look at the latest proofs. That's followed by a quick catch up with the features team. Another day of the week might include breakfast with one of the magazine's commercial partners for a beauty brand.

Once a week Trish fits in a 45-minute spinning class at the gym in the basement of the *Marie Claire* building. Other lunch hours leave her breathless when she attends events such as the launch of Lady Gaga's new perfume, the ingredients of which include 'tears of Belladonna and crushed heart of tiger orchidea'. In fashion, the extraordinary is commonplace. Her afternoons are equally as varied. Trish will review rails of clothes to see what the fashion team are shooting, as well as write cover lines with her team and look at layouts with the art director. With a team of 36 people, the admin side of the job has to be addressed. She may have to deal with flexible working requests, human resources issues and general staff management.

She also meets with the senior team weekly, which includes the publishing director, the marketing manager and members of circulation. They discuss various on-going projects and are updated on what each department is doing. Recently they've spent a lot of time talking about *Marie Claire*'s 25th birthday, which is happening in 2013 and promises some exciting big events. Knowing it would be unfashionable to be late to their own birthday, planning has started well in advance.

À la mode

Her career is, of course, only one aspect of her life and as a mother of twin boys, Trish knows prioritisation is essential. She's felt the pull of many working mothers, balancing time spent with her family versus out-of-hours work functions and travel. 'I think you have to make the decision that if you're going to have a career, you're going to do it properly, and you're not a bad mother for doing that.' Trish is eager to be a positive role model to her sons and teach them the importance of doing something you love for a living.

Something has had to give, however, and looking back, she would say she saw friends less than she might have done. 'I don't feel like I've sacrificed anything, probably more compromised.' She has to be strict with her time to make sure her work and home lives don't bleed into each other. Fortunately her children's school is two minutes away from her home, so she drops them off two or three mornings a week, still making it to the office for 9.30am. For mornings where she has breakfast meetings, this has to be rearranged. 'I'm very disciplined for making sure I'm home for 6.30pm when my nanny is due to leave, so I can spend time with the children before they go to bed. It's the sort of job where, if you wanted, you could be at some fabulous event every night of the week.'

Trish is eager to be a positive role model to her sons and teach them the importance of doing something you love for a living.

She finds being selective about the events she goes to is key. To decide, she considers how the event will impact the brand of *Marie Claire*. Recently she attended the launch of the Empowering Women Awards, a campaign where *Marie Claire* is partnered with Avon against domestic violence. 'I'm not going to deny it: you get invited to the most incredible things and meet the most amazing people. That's all wonderful, but there is a lot of hard work. We go to the fashion collections and of course it's glamorous and fun, but you're literally on the go from 9am to midnight by the time you've finished your last dinner or party. You have to look fabulous, smile and be charming for 15 hours straight. But hey, what a way to spend a day!'

It's the variety of the role – the parties, networking, catwalks and fashion shoots – which is both the joy and the frustration for Trish. 'It's really important you don't allow your diary to be filled with events because then you don't have the time to do the job you're actually there for, which is editing the magazine.'

Haute couture

Outside of work, Trish has plenty going on, including being a judge at the 7th Annual Scottish Fashion Awards. The tartan red carpet played host to a fashion extravaganza which featured nominee catwalk shows, music acts and a runway show that previewed the winter collection of a Paris-based creative director. Hosted by television presenter and model Alexa Chung and judged by representatives for Ralph Lauren, *Vogue* and Vivienne Westwood to name a few, Trish was in well-dressed company.

She is also patron of the Rainbow Trust, a charity to support families of children with either terminal or life-threatening illnesses. A friend had written to ask her to be on the committee for a ball and Trish wanted to use her many contacts in high places to get more involved with the charity. Having just had her twins, the work of the Rainbow Trust struck home and she was excited to start fundraising.

In 2011, she helped organise a VIP catwalk show with Sadie Frost. The Rainbow Trust teamed up with *Marie Claire*, Mywardrobe.com and a couple of other designers, with Storm as the model agency. 'We had Cara Delevingne and Jourdan Dunn, proper international catwalk models.' The night brought the charity to a different audience, outside of its regular contributors. 'It was fantastic, but obviously very nerve-wracking organising the show with Sadie Frost.'

Raison d'être

For those with the same passion for hard work in exchange for unbelievable opportunities, Trish recommends a strong qualification in journalism to gain a competitive edge, as well as building up a portfolio to show a hunger for writing. She warns against the passive act of just saying you want to be a writer. 'With the rise of the web and with newspaper sales down, if you want to be a journalist you have to read newspapers and have heroes: people whose writing you admire.' This can then be a good talking point at interview.

When applying for editorial jobs, 'it's about being fearless'. Trish is often exasperated at the number of letters she gets where a find and replace has been done for the editor's name. A bespoke letter speaks volumes. 'Refer to things in the magazine that impressed you or spoke to you. You have to show a real understanding of the publication and its audience.'

For budding features writers, 'learning to do news gathering is so important. Any experience you can get in the news is really useful'.

Trish is in her third year with *Marie Claire* and the pace has not slowed. 'The magazine sales are doing well, we've just launched *Marie Claire* runway, we've got apps happening and our website, so it really is fabulous here.'

Anticipating a big change in as little as five years' time due to the move to digital, Trish isn't sure how her career fits into this, but wants to stay involved with the industry. From the small-scale of putting a spread together to the full management of the magazine and its departments, her enthusiasm for editorial hasn't waned. Whatever her next step, Trish takes with her everything she has learned throughout her career – how to layout pages, how to manage a team, how to correct a grammar mistake and how to organise a catwalk event – all in a designer handbag, of course.

FOOD CREATIVE

Rachel Khoo

Current title: food creative and television chef

Age and DOB: 32 (b. 1980)

First job: babysitting

Other careers: fashion PR and marketing, au pair, bookseller, caterer, food writer and consultant

Most well known for: her debut cookbook in the UK and BBC television series, both entitled *The Little Paris Kitchen*

Working from a very small but immaculately laid out kitchen, Rachel Khoo burst onto the British food scene like a breath of fresh air early in 2012 with her UK debut cookbook, *The Little Paris Kitchen*, and its accompanying BBC television series. Her immediate popularity may be attributed to her vintage style, bubbly personality and chatty way of demystifying the revered, daunting world of French cookery. What makes her success more extraordinary is that a woman in her mid-twenties from Croydon took the risky decision to move away from a 'safe' London job into the unknown, driven only by passion and an unshakeable work ethic.

Early years

Born in Croydon as the daughter of a Malay/Chinese father and Austrian mother, Rachel's childhood was culturally 'a little different' to a classic British one. She 'grew up with Saturday being spent with the BBCs' – as she called them, the British Born Chinese – and was heavily influenced by Chinese culture socially as well as at home. Her father 'instilled the Chinese work ethic of working hard and was quite strict' whereas her mother 'always encouraged me to be creative and I was always doing scrap books and painting and making things'.

As a teenager, Rachel's family moved to south Germany and she was sent to a local convent school in Bavaria. It was there that she studied for the Mittlere Reife (the German equivalent of GSCEs), in German! 'I had to integrate with Germans, learn the language and pass my GCSEs. It wasn't easy but that's all helped me develop who I am now. I would certainly recommend to anybody to live in another country and experience another culture and learn another language'. It was her time in Germany, a diverse home life and summer holidays spent in Austria that allowed Rachel to become 'open to different cultures at an early age'.

'I would certainly recommend to anybody to live in another country and experience another culture and learn another language'

Returning to the UK for her A levels in Art, Theatre Studies and German, Rachel's childhood creativity was resurfacing and she enrolled in Art and Design at Central Saint Martins College. There she developed a passion for design and got to grips with the commercial side of 'communicating an idea and expressing it in a well-thought-out manner so your audience understands what you're saying'. In having the opportunity to learn about the market side of creativity Rachel thought she had decided to pursue a career in graphic design but it was an experience during a part-time job at college that opened her eyes to food from a professional point of view. 'Through work experience I got a job working as an assistant to a freelance interior stylist. It was on set for a shoot with *The Sunday Times Style Magazine* where I met and assisted a food stylist ... I had always liked cooking at home but in terms of the professional side it sparked an interest in food styling.'

'Typical' graduate

Like many graduates who wish to enter into a creative industry, Rachel found it almost impossible to get work as a food stylist that was paid: 'I lost count of the number of CVs I sent off. In order to stand out within the saturated graduate market Rachel added some flair to her applications: 'I made my CV into a recipe and said something like "These are all the ingredients that make up who I am ..." so I tried to put a creative spin on my CV because that's who I am, I like to do something a little original.' It wasn't long before an employment agency managed to find a suitable placement for her, the first vaguely within a creative environment – data entry within the web marketing department at British fashion house Thomas Pink.

As a foray into the working world, it wasn't the most exciting job – 'people would order something off the website, I would then have to print off the order and manually input it into another system' – but it wasn't long before Rachel was able to make it her own. With the department going through a change, Rachel grabbed the chance to put herself forward for new opportunities – helping with photo-shoots or couriering shirts to certain celebrities for example – utilising the opportunity to 'enrich the job I was already doing'. With her enthusiasm and industrious attitude, Rachel soon progressed within her department – in fact she made herself so busy that when she left her job as e-marketing and public relations (PR) assistant, it was split into three!

With the department going through a change, Rachel grabbed the chance to put herself forward for new opportunities.

But being busy doesn't necessarily equate to job satisfaction. Despite working in a relatively interesting and varied environment Rachel felt that she wasn't using all her skills, the job 'didn't feel creative enough'. Once again her interest in food and food styling began to come to the forefront of her thinking and she felt it was the time to make that leap forward – 'What is exciting about today is that you don't have to feel like "Oh I graduated from university and now I have to do this job for the rest of my life"'. Having lived in and around London for a long time Rachel was also getting the urge to travel, 'I felt that if I didn't move away from London then I would spend the rest of my life in London', so in 2005 she decided, at the age of 25, to combine the two and make a change for the better.

En français s'il vous plait . . .

In search of a career with food, in particular with patisserie, there was nowhere better to start than with a course at the famous Le Cordon Bleu cookery school. The easy option would have been to go to the London branch or even a cookery school in Vienna, where they have a strong patisserie culture and a familiar language but Rachel chose Paris. Why? 'The best patisserie in the world is still Paris – it's got a rich history in patisserie and if you come to Paris every neighbourhood has several amazing patisseries. But also it was because Paris was the tougher job – I didn't know anybody, I didn't speak French – and I like the idea of a challenge and discovering something new.' Initially the plan was to be in France for a year, 'learn French, do Le Cordon Bleu then come back to London and have another shot at getting back into the food styling world'.

One may be forgiven for believing that this decision was just 'an adventure made on a whim' but Rachel freely admits that she's not the typical 'gap year' traveller. 'I like to travel with the sense of having a mission, that you're going to learn something and benefit from it', and so in choosing Paris Rachel would develop her language skillset and gain some much needed experience in food.

Leaving her well-paid PR job in the city to move to a foreign country was a risky move and, financially, Rachel was on her own. 'I put myself through everything; nothing was funded by my parents. They didn't buy me a fabulous flat in Paris, I live in the small apartment from the show – it's not glamorous but I make do with what I have. I got a job as an au pair during my time at Le Cordon Bleu which was a step down from working in fashion PR and marketing'. It was a daunting experience changing careers, but at

Le Cordon Bleu she wasn't alone in her quest: 'There were people in my class who were 40 changing careers and I thought that was really tough!'

From trained chef to food creative

After graduating with a diploma in patisserie, Rachel's venture into cooking was a slow burner. 'It took me a good three years to actually get to the state where I could live off what I was doing with food professionally. The first three years in Paris I was au pairing, I taught English, I worked in a department store selling perfume. I had countless jobs to pay the bills.' Rachel quickly learnt that, in Paris, it was all about who you knew and she tried to crack the book market as a way of making contacts but French publishers 'didn't respond to any of my cold calling'. In her spare time though she was writing an online blog (RKhooks.net) and doing some food styling – helping photographers develop their portfolios whilst Rachel developed hers – this was again unpaid and it all began to get frustrating. 'I was doing all these non-directional jobs and I began to think "I'm 27, why I am I doing this when I have a good degree, had a good job in London, what am I thinking?!" but something in me always thought I'll just give myself another six months. I had this feeling that something was going to come, a glimmer of hope almost that I clung onto'.

It wasn't long before that glimmer became a beacon. In May 2007 she took a job at La Cocotte, a Parisian cookery bookshop. It was there that Rachel baked cakes and biscuits for the salon du thé, catered the book launches and designed quirky cookery classes such as 'Pimp my Cupcake' and 'British Teatime' to tempt Parisian pupils. 'Being in that location, even though it was minimum wage, meant that I started to meet people in the food industry of Paris. By meeting these people I started to get paid jobs, not brilliantly paid but it was something! It paid for the ingredients at least!'

It certainly was true that in Paris it came down to who you know, and Rachel made sure she was in the right place at the right time, proving her talent and passion. 'I think something I learnt from both my parents was that nothing comes from nothing, that you don't earn anything from sitting around. You've got to make it happen yourself and work hard'.

'I had this feeling that something was going to come, a glimmer of hope almost that I clung onto.'

Working with new people meant that Rachel had the chance to grab fresh opportunities. Her friend Marc Grossman, an American food chef and owner of a vegetarian restaurant, introduced her to a food consultant from Volkswagen who was looking for something only Rachel could offer, a chef who spoke German and could make American-style cakes! She was hired as a food consultant for Volkswagen, working for four years on a yearly Christmas patisserie and researching ideas for the German site restaurant, La Coccinella, in 2011. It wasn't long before she expanded her client list and was working with a variety of brands, corporations and venues. 'It's partly putting yourself out there and building that network. I started getting consultancy work, I worked at the bookshop, I started to work on books and then eventually my freelance work was enough to sustain me, so I gave up the bookshop and things grew from there'.

'It's partly putting yourself out there and building that network.'

Food as a passport

Suddenly her career in food was taking Rachel all over the world with new projects, collaborations and 'pop-up restaurants'. It all began when

Rachel set up Edible Tales - a 'pop-up restaurant' venture that would take her all over the world.

she met, by chance, Michelin Star chef Nuno Mendes when they were both working at a food festival in Deauville, Normandy. He told Rachel that he was planning to open up his apartment in London as a supper club to be hosted by a variety of chefs from all over the world. After impressing Nuno in their brief meeting, Rachel was invited to host at The Loft for the evening: 'He gave me the opportunity to put myself out there and it gave me a taste of creating these events. I didn't just think about the food, I collaborated with the designers about table decor and the DJs about music – it was a really creative project for me.' This all-encompassing way of hosting triggered both the designer and chef in Rachel and she was inspired to emulate Nuno's model herself. She started running events all over the world, with customers paying to indulge in 'Edible Tales' in Buenos Aries, Melbourne and Sydney and to experience a tasty way of 'Tearing down the Wall' in Berlin. 'I liked the idea of just doing one or two nights somewhere, doing something original, and then after two nights it's all dismantled and it's gone! I get bored, I think that's the problem with me and I think that's why I could never work in or run a restaurant 9-5.'

Books, books, books

When back in Paris, Rachel was approached once more by her friend Marc Grossman, this time to help test recipes for his new cookbook. Upon completion of the book, 'his editor, who I had previously approached and never heard from, suddenly called me and said, "Look Rachel, we like your work – would you be interested in writing two cookbooks for us?"' Rachel jumped at the opportunity and suddenly had two French language cook-books – *Barres de céréales: Muesli & Granola* and *Je fais mes pâtes à tartiner* – published in 2010 by Marabout. It seemed that her determination and strong work ethic coupled with starting to know people in the industry was paying off.

By September 2010 Rachel had had an idea for a new book, this time for a British audience. She wanted to break down the cliché of complicated French cookery and teach British urbanites with 'normal' kitchens 'French food the way Parisians cook and eat'. With the longstanding British love affair of Italian cookery, Rachel felt that by demonstrating the ease of the everyday French meal, she could trigger a new passion on the British scene. 'Unlike France, where I had to know somebody, in the UK I just sent my favourite publishers proposal emails and out of the 15 I contacted, three agreed to meet with me – Penguin, Hodder and Stoughton and

Ebury'. One rejected her idea outright, another considered it but was reluctant because Rachel had no media presence in the UK, but Penguin loved 'The Little Paris Kitchen' idea, said 'Yes', and she signed with them in November 2010. Having secured a book deal, Rachel was suddenly faced with the intimidating task of compiling 120 recipes . . .

The smallest restaurant in Paris

It wasn't the scale of recipes that Rachel deemed the main concern of the new book; it was the food waste that would be generated in testing them. Having past experience in big, international pop-ups Rachel suddenly realised that she could scale down the operation to her 21m² apartment in the centre of Paris with only two gas rings, a little oven and 'a table for two'. Et voila! La Petite Cuisine à Paris was born! What she needed now were willing restaurant guests and, being on a tight budget, she utilised her PR and marketing skills.

'Luckily we live in an age of the internet which allows us to find ways to communicate, find cheap ways of doing things ourselves' so instead of advertising in newspapers or flyering, Rachel used her social media networks as a food writer – her blog, Twitter and Facebook page – to attract people for the project. Finding your way in a minefield of social media can be difficult when starting new ventures but Rachel found that in taking your

Rachel in her 'Little Paris Kitchen'.

time and keeping focus you can prosper – 'It's about putting something of quality out there, quality is key.' So unique was her proposal that people responded within 20 seconds of posting! Her miniscule restaurant soon became the place to eat for foodies in Paris and given that she's an English girl doing French cuisine in the heart of the capital, that wasn't bad!

Finding your way in a minefield of social media can be difficult when starting new ventures but Rachel found that in taking your time and keeping focus you can prosper.

Everywhere but the UK

'I set up my home restaurant to primarily test my recipes but also, coming from a marketing/PR background, I knew journalists are always looking for stories and I thought – even if it's just underground – it would generate a little interest.' Little did she know just how many people would take an interest! The story of the smallest kitchen in Paris became a huge trend on Twitter and, not long afterwards, it was picked up by the international press. Newspapers in Japan, Italy, Brazil, Australia and New York were reporting on the global news story that was Rachel Khoo and her pint-size restaurant. The only place, it seemed, where word hadn't spread was the UK. 'It didn't really get picked up in the UK which was funny because at the same time I was approaching production companies in the UK about doing a TV project' – she was going to make the Brits sit up and take notice one way or another.

Creating a spectacle

With the test kitchen set up and the book starting to come together, Rachel began to approach production companies in early 2011. 'I wasn't desperate to do TV but I felt the book would make a good TV series so I went to quite a few production companies – all the big ones – until I found a small, independent who immediately understood the premise and loved it.' With a firm hand on the concept, Rachel pitched successfully to Plum Pictures and they agreed to shoot a taster in April 2011.

Crammed into her tiny kitchen with microphones and cameras, Rachel's only instruction was to 'cook' – 'I didn't get any training so what you see is who I am.' Understanding the need for a 'hook' with cookery shows, Rachel knew that as a woman she would be taken on face value and that her vintage style and looks would attract some audience members. But she was determined not to over-sexualise the food in the same way some female chefs have in the past – 'You have to be media friendly but in the end people will always go back to the book and it's still quality work, they are great recipes. I want to be able to look back in 10 years' time and still be happy and proud of it and I think I will be.'

With the taster done, it was time to hit the networks. Much in the same way as the book, Rachel was met with mixed reactions – one channel said 'no' but the BBC, though initially hesitant, came back with the offer of a pilot. This was commissioned in August 2011, presented in October and then immediately commissioned as a six-part series for the 2012 spring programming. 'It was absolutely extraordinary! The production company has worked in the industry for many years and they said that it's unheard of that someone unknown is given the opportunity for a primetime show. I think I just had the right timing and a good story to tell, a story of hard work at the end of the day. When I told my Mum about the TV deal her reaction was "What?! Who wants to see you on telly, you're normal!"'

Big things from small kitchens

Despite being just 'normal', the reaction to Rachel has been astonishing. For a country that was seemingly the last to discover her, the UK really took to *The Little Paris Kitchen* and its chef. After the showing of the first episode on BBC2 in March 2012, Rachel's Twitter followers reached the thousands and within the first two months of release, her book sold well over 50,000 copies. As well as holding the top spot on the Amazon cookery book chart, *The Little Paris Kitchen* also reached the top five on the Amazon bestsellers list behind blockbuster fiction like *The Hunger Games*. 'It's been amazing in the fact that I was unknown in the UK and all these projects have been initiated by me and they've been something I've really believed in and been behind.'

Courage and passion led Rachel to Paris and self-belief took her ideas to the next level of international travel, professional cooking and a media presence with a second English language cookbook already in the pipeline. Moving to a foreign country and completely immersing yourself in the culture is incredibly daunting for anyone. But Rachel firmly believes that: 'If you want to develop yourself as a chef you should go round all the best kitchens in the world. The more you expose yourself to different cuisines, the richer your background and own cuisine, and even life, will be.' If you have a passion for something at the end of the day 'nobody is ever going to work as hard as you' to fulfil it so try something small and you never know who you might meet or where the road will take you.

GENRE WRITER

Barbara Machin

Current title: TV screenwriter

First job: promotional scriptwriter for Granada

Other careers: teaching

Most well known for: writing and creating *Waking the Dead*

Barbara Machin grew up wanting to be a writer, however she had no contacts to ask for advice and no idea of how to get into the industry. When an opening for a promotional scriptwriter at Granada Television was advertised, lacking any knowledge of what the role involved, Barbara decided that any job description with the word 'writer' had to be a step forward. Through this experience, Barbara soon learned that any opportunity related to her dream should be seized and while she did not immediately get the chance to write, she had made a strategic move in the right direction. While Barbara had many opportunities to be successful in other fields, through always holding onto her childhood dream, she eventually reached her goal of becoming a writer and is today the proud owner of an Emmy Award for her television series, *Waking the Dead*.

The imperfect plan

With the plan of becoming a writer, Barbara Machin attended Hull University after leaving school, where she read English and drama. Yet on leaving the university, she realised she had no idea how to make it in the field, no one to advise her and as yet, no way of making money. Consequently, Barbara moved to Manchester to study for her postgraduate degree and become a teacher, all the while thinking: 'Well what I'll do is become a teacher, because I don't mind the thought of that, and in the long holidays, I will write my great opus.' However, Barbara soon discovered that this plan had one major flaw: 'Teaching, although an exhilarating career, left no time for writing at all.'

Consequently Barbara started to look for ways of achieving her dream career and while continuing to teach she entered a local Young Writer of the Year Award, which involved writing an interesting article on a famous person and a piece of travel writing. Winning the competition gave Barbara the push she needed to believe in her writing ability and she started to look for jobs that better suited her passion: 'That was my turning point. I think that's one of the commonalities as a writer, you need someone to look at you and say, "Oh, you're good, you could do this". In 1976 Barbara noticed an advert for a promotional scriptwriter with Granada Television and, as mentioned above, despite having no idea what the role involved, she decided to apply as it at least had the word 'writer' in the job description. Originally, Barbara had hoped to become a novelist, however, gaining acceptance into the Granada apprenticeship gave her an amazing entry point into the world of television, where she would eventually learn her talent for genre scriptwriting.

Discovering her trade

The promotional scriptwriter role involved writing trailers, as well as learning how to put together and edit pictures on the screen, providing Barbara with the confidence to start writing for television. After a year in the promotion department, Barbara decided to apply for a job within Granada that would allow her more time to write and she managed to obtain a job writing for a consumer affairs programme, which was aired for around 20 minutes per week. Soon Barbara's success with this project led to Granada extending the show to 30 minutes per week and her role developed as she started to research for, write and present the show. Unfortunately, this meant that she still did not have the time to work on her personal writing, however, the experience served to build up her confidence in the world of television and gave her valuable material that she could use in her writing at a later date.

Barbara found that once she had her foot in the door at Granada, there was an amazing opportunity for movement within the television company and she managed to obtain a job with Granada Reports, presenting the news on the main desk. At the same time, Granada opened a studio in Liverpool, and Barbara became the anchor there, creating a film a day, 'covering everything from the Yorkshire Ripper through to the general elections'. Yet, once again while she was very interested in what she was doing, Barbara was in a job that did not leave her any time to write. Using the flexibility of Granada Television to her advantage, Barbara left the world of television journalism and moved to the drama department, where she became an associate drama producer for shows such as *Coronation Street, Crown Court* and *Brideshead Revisited*. Working with directors and writers, Barbara was able to learn the craft of scriptwriting. Moreover, the role taught her exactly how and to whom she should pitch her own written scripts and soon she had two of her own television productions made by Granada.

Barbara's early experiences at Granada helped build her confidence in the world of television and gave her valuable material that she could use in her writing at a later date.

After two years as an associate drama producer, Barbara decided that it was time to push for her career in writing and she applied for the role of arts council writer-in-residence in Ipswich in 1983. Barbara's application was successful and her new role involved encouraging children to enjoy writing, while also finally giving her the time she needed to write, as half of her hours were dedicated solely to this occupation. Placed in a 'tough' school in Nacton, Ipswich, Barbara found the career change a struggle: 'the kids pretty much ate the flesh off my bones', nonetheless Barbara finally felt that she was moving in the right direction. 'That was the first time that I dared to think of myself as writer because I had as my title "writer-in-residence".'

Taking the leap

After Barbara's year-long residency, her writing finally took off and she began to receive commissions for her work. She wrote a play for the Library Theatre and one for the Royal Exchange in Manchester and she also received her first television commission, to write for a daytime soap made by Thames Television called *Gems*: 'That felt like an enormous leap, because although I wasn't yet making a proper living writing, I was getting things made. Other people were regarding me as a writer, and I had an agent.' Barbara spent the next five years taking any commissions that came her way, whether they were for radio, television, theatre or even short stories for anthologies, yet she knew by this point that her passion lay with screenwriting. During this time, Barbara was still failing to make a successful living from writing alone and so she took on a sideline career as a photographer. While Barbara was earning more money through her photography than her writing, she was never persuaded to drop her passion for the extra cash and she continued to take any job that related to her writing, which included working for the Arts Council as a literature fieldworker for Suffolk, organising book and poetry groups.

While Barbara was earning more money through her photography than her writing, she was never persuaded to drop her passion for the extra cash.

Soon, Barbara began to receive regular commissions to write for shows such as *Casualty* and *The Bill* and she continues to view similar long-running shows as a great starting place for aspiring writers, as it's where she was able to learn the tough skill of portraying her own voice, despite writing for someone else's show. Moreover, writing for such shows gave her the opportunity to work among the people she would work with in the future as a writer of her own show: 'During that period I was not only learning my craft as a writer, and enjoying the fabulous process and the nightmare process of getting stuff on the screen, but also forging the links that would allow me to do my own stuff as well alongside that.'

Writing reality

During this time, Barbara discovered her passion for genre writing, enjoying becoming immersed in another world of law, medicine or crime throughout the writing process. Barbara's journalistic experience proved invaluable during this time, having taught her the investigative skill and love of research that is a vital part of this writing style: 'If you shortcut the research, you stop the real and vivid authenticity coming out of your writing.' Barbara's research involved directly working with people within various careers and riding in rapid response cars or spending time on hospital wards, and encouraged her to become excited about the field of her writing, thus fuelling her creativity.

Nonetheless, Barbara explains that the key ingredient to her skill is imagination: 'It's probably 70% imagination. You can research all you like, but it won't create great stories or great characters.' Barbara's other form of research in the early stages of her career involved simply watching similar medical and crime dramas to see how other writers coped with writing about the technical side of different occupations without overcomplicating matters for viewers. Through watching programmes such as *ER*, Barbara learned that while it is important to be authentic, a certain degree of poetic licence is necessary to simplify the content, such as occasionally extending a character's responsibilities far beyond the reality of their occupation.

After spending most of the 1990s receiving regular commissions to write for long-runners, Barbara felt ready to concentrate on her real dream of creating her own television series. This was a significant gamble for Barbara, as it meant turning down freelance work for five months, to give herself the time to write. During this period, Barbara created around 24 different ideas for television shows and pitched them to commissioning editors and producers at the BBC. She discovered that persistence was a key asset during this time, as it was not until her 24th pitch that people began to show an interest. The successful pitch would become the award-winning series, *Waking the Dead*, which aimed to focus on a multi-disciplinary team of police, detectives and forensics.

In 1999 when Barbara wrote the pilot, detective series tended to concentrate on a single protagonist and *Waking the Dead* was thus viewed by commissioners as an extremely innovative concept. Consequently, Barbara feels that in order to create a successful series, 'You obviously need a great idea, but you also need great timing.' The show was piloted as two single-hour shows on consecutive nights and Barbara had to wait a further year before the show was commissioned for a whole series in 2000. The series was an amazing hit and was soon aired on BBC America, UKTV in Australia and New Zealand and ABC1 in Australia. Four years later, *Waking the Dead*'s success across the globe was made evident, when the show won an International Emmy Award for best drama and the series continued to entertain viewers until 2009: 'Writing for long series is an astonishing job, and making something last nine years is quite something.'

Barbara discovered that persistence was a key asset, as it was not until her 24th pitch that people began to show an interest.

Old dog new tricks

During her nine years with *Waking the Dead*, Barbara saw her career developing from the early days of writing for long-runners. Working in a more executive role, Barbara was able to determine the budget and she asked for a fee to be allocated to advisors, including doctors and policemen, to help her to maintain the show's authenticity. Consequently, she has accumulated a team of professionals that she is able to call on for advice today and she continues to insist on a fee for such advisors. Moreover, while writing a successful television series involved a great deal of responsibility, Barbara found that some of the pressure that comes with writing for other people's shows had actually been reduced, as she could work to a more acceptable timescale with her own show. Furthermore, Barbara explains that writing for a pre-designed character can be more challenging than working on your own creation. Nonetheless, she feels that any good writer can use the opportunity to write for long-runners to channel their own creativity, despite the tight constraints: 'Even when working on long-runners or soaps you should remain creative and optimistic and idealistic at all times. If you don't then you shouldn't be a writer for television.'

With this in mind, Barbara was extremely excited in 2006, when she was asked to write a two-part Christmas special for *Casualty*, after nearly 10 years away from the hospital-based series. Barbara was particularly honoured to be commissioned for the project, as the show was set to mark the 21st anniversary of the series and she saw this as an ideal time to shake up some of the tight writing constraints of the long-runner. Barbara ran backwards and forwards across time during the episodes, telling the same story through three different angles, something that the 21-year-old show had never tried before: 'It was a perfect storm, and you very rarely feel totally pleased with something.'

'Even when working on long-runners or soaps you should remain creative and optimistic and idealistic at all times.'

Generation gap

Today, Barbara gives many guest lectures at universities, for students studying her craft. When Barbara was starting as a writer, television companies would often commission more work than they could use, which meant that writers would receive the money and the experience, even if the show did not make it to the air. She feels that this is the key change to the field since the economic crash, as companies can no longer afford to over-commission, giving aspiring writers fewer opportunities to write. Nonetheless, far more shows are produced today than ever before and while *Casualty* aired just 12 programmes a year when Barbara first worked for the series, there are now 48 produced annually. Consequently, she feels that with the right amount of determination, it is still possible to succeed in the world of genre screenwriting today: 'you just have to be dogged as hell and as inventive as you can be to keep exposing what you do to the people that make these shows.'

Alongside advising up-and-coming writers, Barbara continues to write for genre television. She is currently working on a programme about profilers and she has enjoyed immersing herself in the world of psychology and psychiatry, recently visiting a locked ward in a psychiatric unit to gain the all-important research. Through completely submerging into the world of their show, Barbara believes that any aspiring writer can produce work for genre television: 'Ultimately none of us are doctors or policeman but we can imagine ourselves into it with the right fuel in the tank. It's just about capturing the red-bloodedness of life.'

ICHTHYOLOGIST
Dr Eugenie Clark

Current title: senior research scientist and professor emerita at the University of Maryland; senior research scientist and founding director at the Mote Marine Laboratory

Age and DOB: 90 (b. 1922)

First job: dog walker for wealthy New York residents whilst studying at Hunter College

Other careers: published author, university professor

Most well known for: being a world-renowned authority on sharks

Dr Eugenie 'Genie' Clark has achieved more in her lifetime than most people could ever imagine. The American ichthyologist, whose extensive and often groundbreaking studies of fish have earned her the title 'The Shark Lady', is still going strong in a career which has spanned an incredible eight decades. Despite marrying five times, raising four children and battling lung cancer, Genie has never given up on her determination to live her dream.

Entering the patriarchal world of science in the 1940s, the intrepid Genie studied to doctorate level at New York University, travelled the world to conduct 82 deep submersible dives, established the Mote Marine Laboratory in Florida and taught at the University of Maryland for 32 years, while also finding the time to write three books and nearly 300 scientific and popular articles. She has received international recognition in the form of three honorary doctoral degrees, the Gold Medal Award from the Society of Women Geographers, the President's Medal from the University of Maryland and countless awards, including those from the National Geographic Society, the Explorers Club and the Underwater Society of America. Most recently, in March 2010, she was inducted into the Florida Women's Hall of Fame by the Governor of Florida. Now aged 90, this tenacious and eternally inquisitive woman remains very much active in her field, showing how a passion ignited in childhood can continue to burn throughout a lifetime.

Underwater aspirations

Born in New York on 4 May 1922, Genie was raised by her Japanese mother Yumico after her American father Charles died when she was just a baby. One fateful day, when Genie was 9 years old, the close mother and daughter duo took a trip from their small apartment in Long Island to the New York Aquarium in Battery Park. Stepping into the aquatic haven, the young Genie was overcome by the surrounding sights and, in her own words, 'became fascinated with the idea that you could keep an aquarium in your house and have these fishes alive that you could watch 24/7'. From that day forward, her life would never be the same. Destiny had intervened and worked its magic, capturing Genie's heart and mind, and mapping out her lifelong career path. 'If it hadn't been for a public aquarium when I was nine years old then I might never have gone into this field and I don't know what I would have done.'

With her passion for the underwater world firmly established, little Genie immersed herself in marine biology books, collected her own fish at

A young Genie with her mother, Yumico.

home and became an avid follower of her childhood hero William Beebe, a popular American scientist of the early 20th century. Listening to radio accounts of Beebe's deep sea dive off the coast of Bermuda in the bathysphere, Genie fervently hoped that she would grow up to follow in his footsteps.

Genie's mother worked on Saturday mornings at a newspaper stand in the Downtown Athletic Club of Lower Manhattan and Genie would have to sit behind the counter. When Yumico had finished work, she would take Genie to the nearby Battery Park Aquarium. After becoming acquainted with the guards, Genie asked her mother if she could spend her Saturday mornings at the aquarium instead of behind the newspaper stand. From then on, Genie whiled away her time at the nearby aquarium, gazing at the fish she loved so dearly. As a regular attendee, Genie developed a 'group of friends'– caretakers, guards and visitors – whom she entertained with the scientific facts she had gleaned from her beloved books. And it was these Saturday sojourns, spent perched upon the edge of the shark tank, which were of paramount importance in the formation of her long-term aspirations. 'I used to climb on the railing, get my nose practically on the glass, look in and pretend that I was diving with sharks. I thought, "God, I'd love to do this someday; to actually get underwater and look at sharks and marine fishes".'

Schooling

Throughout her years at grammar school and high school, Genie ardently pursued her interest in biology, blissfully unaware of the opposition that she would encounter. In the late 1930s, as the time arrived for Genie to decide what she wished to study at college, the intellectual pool of science was, unfortunately, one in which women rarely dipped their toes. Aware of Genie's intention to break with convention and step into a man's world, her family expressed concern. 'They said "Shouldn't you take up typing so you can become a secretary to some scientist who works with fishes?" And I said "I don't want to be a secretary to somebody who studies fishes; I want to study fishes myself." So I never took up typing.'

Resilient against the inherent sexism of the era and resolutely determined to turn her fascination for fish into a successful career, Genie enrolled at Hunter College in New York to major in zoology. Attending summer schools at the University of Michigan Biological Station, she accelerated her studies and obtained her Bachelor of Arts at the age of 20. Graduating in the midst of the Second World War, Genie was unable to secure work in biology, but having taken many optional chemistry modules as part of her degree, she was qualified to make her first foray into science, working as a chemist at the Celanese Corporation, a plastics company in New Jersey.

Unable to give up on her underwater aspirations, Genie applied for graduate school at Columbia University but found herself subjected to the prejudices of the interviewing professor, who told Genie that she would probably get married, have children and fail to pursue her career. Undeterred by his discouragement, Genie began to work towards her Master's in zoology at New York University, where the head of the Department of Zoology, Professor Charipper, warmly welcomed her. It was at this point in her life that Genie met her tutor Dr Charles M. Breder, the curator of the Department of Ichthyology at the American Museum of Natural History, and the man who Genie credits as the 'greatest influence' in her career; a 'friend, teacher and mentor'. Unlike many people Genie encountered, Dr Breder considered the notion of a woman entering marine biology to be an appropriate and refreshing change. 'He taught me a lot about fishes and encouraged me to study them, not for how much money you could make or what kind of job you could have, but just to learn about fishes.'

Diving in

After achieving her Master of Arts in 1946, the tirelessly hardworking Genie embarked upon her first position as a research assistant at the Scripps Institution of Oceanography in San Diego. A year later, Genie returned to New York to become a research assistant in the Department of Animal Behavior at the American Museum of Natural History, a role which also provided the opportunity to work towards her PhD in zoology. Reflecting upon her career choices, Genie believes that following the academic route into her profession enabled her to gain invaluable experiences. 'It was a big advantage for me to study for a doctor's degree because then I could apply for fellowships and scholarships.'

One fortuitous day, whilst undertaking research for her doctoral thesis, the student Genie stumbled upon two announcements in the museum library; the first offering the chance to win a Fulbright Scholarship to study abroad, whilst the second was advertising for an ichthyologist to join the Office of Naval Research and explore the newly acquired Trust Territories in the Pacific. Applying for both positions, with little hope of securing either, Genie was amazed when, in 1949, she found herself setting off to study plectognaths and poisonous fish in Micronesia, before moving on, in 1950, to investigate the same species in Egypt's Red Sea for her Fulbright Scholarship. 'I had a wonderful time travelling and a great start to my career because I had the opportunity to go to both these places.'

'It was a big advantage for me to study for a doctor's degree because then I could apply for fellowships and scholarships.'

When she returned from her overseas adventures, Genie was approached by Elizabeth Lawrence, an editor at Harper and Brothers publishers, who was impressed by a short article she had written for *Natural History Magazine* in January 1951. Genie confesses: 'I had no idea of writing a book and, in fact, I was sure I couldn't handle it.' As she struggled with self-doubt, Genie turned to her uncle, a faithful supporter who had saved all the letters she sent home while travelling. He encouraged Genie to put pen to paper and share her stories with the world, assuring her that if she adopted the simple writing style of her letters then she could not fail to enchant her readers. With her confidence boosted, an advance on her book, a scholarship to the Bread Loaf Writer's Conference and enthusiastic support from the editors at Harpers, in 1952 Genie completed her first book (a week before she had her first child). *Lady with a Spear*, an autobiographical account of her time in Micronesia and the Red Sea, was a Book-of-the-Month Club selection in America, produced in 23 foreign editions, and catapulted Genie into the public eye, transforming her from an unknown academic into a well-publicised and increasingly sought after authority on the underwater world. 'It was a very successful book, a lot of copies were sold and I made more money than I ever expected to make in a lifetime.'

An ocean of knowledge

Looking back upon the propitious opportunities that seem to have appeared at exactly the right moments in her career, Genie admits: 'I'm a lucky person and things have just come to me.' The summer of 1954 was undoubtedly one of those moments. In Englewood, Florida, the wealthy William and Anne Vanderbilt had become captivated by their young son Bill's collection of aquariums and, having read *Lady with a Spear*, were keen to indulge Bill's passion with a visit from the Lady herself. Enter Genie Clark. Invited down to Englewood to give a small lecture in a private room at the Vanderbilts' estate, Genie soon found herself in a crowded schoolhouse, as residents and fisherman flocked to hear about her adventures in the Red Sea and satisfy their curiosity about fish.

Overwhelmed by the locals' interest in marine biology, the Vanderbilts asked Genie to start a new laboratory; a place for research, learning and enjoyment of all things aquatic. Prior to accepting the position, Genie sought guidance from her trusted advisor Dr Breder, who urged his protégé to seize the opportunity to study the rich, relatively unexplored west coast of Florida. Buoyed by Dr Breder's encouragement and with funding from the generous Vanderbilt family, Genie journeyed to Florida in January 1955 to establish the Cape Haze Marine Laboratory with the help of local fisherman Beryl Chadwick. 'We started in this little wooden building and it was so popular, everybody wanted to come and learn about fishes.'

During her time at the laboratory, Genie dived on a regular basis to observe the fish in their natural habitat, discovering new species and collecting specimens of sharks to keep alive in the laboratory's pool. She undertook experiments to determine the intelligence, feeding habits and reproductive behaviour of sharks. As Cape Haze became renowned for its studies of sharks, Genie's reputation as a fearless female scientist grew, earning her the title 'The Shark Lady'.

'We started in this little wooden building and it was so popular, everybody wanted to come and learn about fishes.'

Genie spent 12 years in Florida nurturing the development of the laboratory, a period of her life which she documented in her second book *The Lady and the Sharks*, published in 1969 by Harper & Row and currently available in its fourth edition from Peppertree Press. From its humble beginnings with two employees and a couple of sharks, the Cape Haze

Genie's extensive experience with sharks has earned her the title 'The Shark Lady'.

Marine Laboratory has evolved into a pioneering research institute; now known as the Mote Marine Laboratory, it boasts hundreds of staff, thousands of volunteers and 400,000 visitors a year.

With such extensive experience in her field, it was almost inevitable that Genie would return to her academic roots and share her knowledge with the new generation of ichthyologists. In 1968, she became a professor in the Department of Zoology at the University of Maryland. For anyone who has had the privilege to encounter Genie, it comes as little surprise that she is widely reported to have been a firm favourite among the university's student population.

'I love teaching and telling people about fishes and how wonderful they are.'

A conversation with Genie offers a veritable feast of anecdotes about her worldwide adventures and any listener, regardless of their previous interest in fish, cannot help but be swept along by her unbounded enthusiasm for the underwater world. Genie's infectious enthusiasm has evidently captured her family as well, as her four children regularly join her for dives and her grandson Eli, at the tender age of five, became the youngest published photographer in *National Geographic*, after his shot of a whale shark was snapped up by the famous magazine.

Making waves

Given Genie's incredible career trajectory and achievements, it is all too easy to forget that her entry into ichthyology was an uphill struggle, a constant battle against the gender conventions of the mid-20th century which designated women as homemakers, while men were free to explore the world. Indomitable as ever, Genie recalls that: 'Even when there was prejudice against women doing this kind of work, I'd squeeze my way in somehow.'

The Shark Lady's passion and perseverance provided her with a passport into the uncharted male territory of science, and she was determined to keep up with her colleagues every step of the way. However, during her studies at the Scripps Institution of Oceanography, Genie was left frustrated by the famous oceanographer Harald Sverdrup's insistence that women were forbidden to attend overnight boat trips. Genie and fellow

Genie's up-close experiences with sharks have given her some remarkable stories to tell.

student Betty Kamp, the only women out of the 30 graduates at the institution, were left behind while the men took 'fascinating trips' to Guadalupe. As the years trickled by, the world of science gradually opened up to women. 'Once they started to give equality to women, they wanted to have a token woman or two on every oceanographic vessel to show that they weren't prejudiced.'

Studying 'sleeping sharks' in a cave off the coast of Cozumel, Mexico, with her graduate student Anita George is one of Genie's most significant memories. As the women were sneaking around the water conducting their investigations, photographers from the *National Geographic* magazine captured on film the spectacle of female scientists bravely confronting one of the most feared creatures. When the cover article 'Into the lairs of "sleeping" sharks' was published in 1975, Genie maintains that she and Anita 'got the most credit because we were women. It kind of balanced out; sometimes it was a disadvantage to be a woman and other times it was almost an unfair advantage that we were doing this because we were women.'

As one of the pioneering female scientists, who forced the world to acknowledge the contributions that 'the fairer sex' can make, Genie proudly declares that women's position in science has 'changed a lot'. When Genie first joined the American Elasmobranch Society at the start of her career, she was one of two women among over a hundred men and now, decades later, over half of the members are female.

Having smashed through the glass ceiling, the Shark Lady has inspired women worldwide over many generations, helping to change the face of science forever.

All rivers flow back to the sea

After 32 years of teaching the ichthyologists of the future at the University of Maryland, Genie migrated back to the Mote Marine Laboratory, purportedly to retire. In reality, Genie has continued to satisfy her insatiable intellectual curiosity, spending her days reading in the 'wonderful library' and writing up all her scientific findings, something

Genie is as passionate now about fish as ever.

which she feels is her responsibility to achieve. 'I don't know if I'll feel well enough to dive anymore but I haven't yet gotten the concept of retiring!'

Perhaps the most inspiring, and arguably enviable, element of Genie's story is the fact that she has managed to make a lifelong career out of something she loves. The Shark Lady's passion for the underwater world, for fish, for swimming and diving, has never waned in over 80 years. Whilst she admits that 'sometimes the work piles up', Genie cannot help but enthuse about her job, admitting that she is 'overwhelmed' by the amount of letters she receives from her admirers, both children and adults alike. 'I've just been very lucky; I've had a lot of good things happen to me and I've never regretted anything I did. I think I've worked hard at it, but I don't really call it work.'

Genie's hard work and extensive contributions to academia have been recognised with over 30 awards throughout her lifetime and she also received three honorary doctor of science degrees in the early 1990s. As she approaches the end of her career, Genie looks forward to the new generation of scientists and believes that 'there are wonderful opportunities now'. She advises those eager to follow in her footsteps to study hard, join relevant societies to keep up to date with the latest scientific findings, and 'take a lot of maths on the side too, whether you like it or not!' And advice from the Shark Lady, who has persisted against the odds to reach an eminent status in her field, is surely worth treasuring. 'Just follow your heart and if you study the things that you love to study then you'll do the best in them.'

MUSICIAN

Johnny Marr

Current title: guitarist and singer

Age and DOB: 48 (b. 1963)

First job: supermarket shelf-stacker

Other careers: visiting professor, session musician

Most well known for: being the guitarist and song-writer for The Smiths

There are few sounds more iconic in British rock music than Johnny Marr's trademark guitar tone. From the jangly introduction to 'This Charming Man', to the dramatic sweep of 'How Soon Is Now?', Johnny's guitar work in The Smiths changed popular music forever. What we now call 'indie' music has its origins in the Manchester group, whose hymns of working-class escapism have personally resonated for decades for would-be rockstars. Put simply, without Johnny Marr and The Smiths, there would be no Oasis, no Arctic Monkeys.

The extent of Johnny's influence is colossal, but unlike many great musical pioneers, he has shown no signs of ever slowing down. Over the years, he has lent his guitar skills to dozens of other projects. His session work for the likes of Pet Shop Boys, Bryan Ferry and even Girls Aloud shows just how in demand he is. With record sales in the millions, and an unrivalled roster of session work to his name, it's safe to say Johnny is at the very top of the music world. However, rockstar clichés are hardly appropriate here. Johnny's down-to-earth and personable manner stem from his inauspicious roots. A Mancunian through and through, his story is one of determination and hard work, driven by his compulsion to get out of working-class suburbia.

Time to daydream

John Martin Maher was born on 31 October 1963 in Ardwick, Manchester. He was the son of two Irish immigrants, who had come over to the UK for a better lot in life. His parents were young and very much into Britain's burgeoning pop culture scene in a way that left a big impression on their son. Coming from a family of music enthusiasts was one important influence on the young John, who would adopt the famous name change in 1983 to distinguish himself from the Buzzcocks' drummer John Maher.

Another important influence was the work ethic that his family background instilled in him: 'I come from a working-class Irish family. They say that the English work to live and the Irish live to work, and I kind of grew up with that sort of ethic really. It was a given that I was going to get a job when old enough.' Johnny would soon put this ethic into practice. After a few paper rounds as a young teen, he took up a job stacking shelves in the Wythenshawe branch of the Co-operative supermarket. 'I was around 15 and it was pretty soul-destroying, but it gave me time to daydream a little bit.' Later, having left school, Johnny took up his first full-time job in a clothes shop, something he describes as 'a related part of the culture of working-class artists, and part of being a musician in waiting'. Fashion has always been important in rock music, and The Smiths were no exception.

Johnny's eyeliner days may be long gone, but the influence his early working life had on his career should not be downplayed. Daydreaming through long weekend shifts at the supermarket and later immersing himself in the fashion side of pop culture all contributed to the development of what, from a young age, had been his biggest aim: to play great rock and roll music.

'I was around 15 and [my job stacking shelves] was pretty soul-destroying, but it gave me time to daydream a little bit.'

An other-worldly connection

Despite growing up in a time when 'the class system in the UK was a lot more prominent', a situation in which 'pursuing the arts was not thought of as a proper job,' Johnny decided from an early age that he would break the expectations of his working-class origins and pursue music full time. 'I just decided at 12 or 13 that the life of a musician was the life for me,' he recalls. 'That was going to be my full-time occupation whether I was poor or not.' This kind of determination to pursue the musician's life, with both its trappings and its risk of failure, exemplifies the passion that the young Johnny felt.

While his early working life simply convinced him that the escape offered by music was worth following, the origins of his love of music reach further back in time. So, whereas other kids would play with more conventional toys, he was given guitars to play with. To this day Johnny maintains that his 'otherworldly aesthetic connection' to the guitar comes from his childhood surroundings. Nonetheless, it was not something he grew out of. Through his teenage years and early working life he would nurture his love of pop music and guitar playing to an almost 'obsessive' degree. 'The first proper guitar I ever got was from a shop that sold mops, brooms and buckets, some really unglamorous kind of place,' Johnny remembers. It was exactly the lack of glamour in his immediate surroundings that helped him focus on his guitar playing.

His early musical influences were diverse, ranging from T-Rex through to dance music. These exact styles aren't particularly evident in his own playing though. As a self-taught musician, he never set out to imitate other guitar players, and he wasn't forced into playing anything he didn't want to, helping him to develop his own unique style more organically. He would spend hours playing obsessively in his bedroom, figuring things out by ear. By his mid-teens it was clear that music was more than just his hobby: 'It started to mean an escape from the mundane world of suburbia. My natural curiosity and ability with the guitar converged with a teenage kind of artistry. I started to really enjoy the poetic aspects of making music.'

'[Music] was going to be my full-time occupation whether I was poor or not.'

Living life in 3D

By the early 1980s, Johnny's experience as a musician had grown significantly through long hours of practising, and regular jam sessions with other young musicians. He soon began to look beyond his own immediate surroundings for ways he could meet the group of people with whom he could reach wider success: 'I was driven to get out of a 2D world and put my 3D glasses on.' While still working his shop-job, he regularly formed bands and sought out other people to play with, but it was clear that to take it to the next level he'd need someone really special. He knew there would be someone out there who shared his vision. He tried every lead he could, taking buses 10 miles out of the city just to meet up with people who seemed like they might have what it took. 'I really put the hours in because I was so focused. But finally I got desperate; desperate enough to knock on a stranger's door.'

That stranger was Stephen Morrissey, an unemployed writer living in Hulme. Johnny got his name through some friends who had played with Morrissey before. It was clear that he was a guy who took himself seriously in terms of his vocals and his lyrics. Before long he and Johnny had hit it off and they started writing songs together. Their fusion of poppy hooks with doom-laden, introspective and poetic lyrics would see them reach international fame.

Johnny had found his vocalist, and The Smiths was born. As co-founders, Stephen and Johnny picked the name because it was the most ordinary, non-pretentious name they could think of. It was part reaction against the contemporary trend for extravagant band names in pop music, and part tribute to their own 'ordinary', working-class roots. The first two songs they wrote, 'Suffer little children' and 'Hand that rocks the cradle,' did not seem to have the kind of commercial appeal needed to make a widespread impact on the music world: 'Until we got that first hit, I was not expecting any cheques to come through the door, but I was still really driven 100%, because I didn't just see it as a job.' But it quickly became Johnny's full-time occupation. He left his job in the clothes shop in 1982 when The Smiths starting gigging. Before this, the job had just been the 'daytime aspect of being a musician,' a means to an end while he found his feet. With The Smiths formed, he had found his calling.

Johnny and Stephen were convinced that their unconventional song-writing and unique style could take them far. Their passionate belief set them in motion: 'I went and tried every lead we could, tried everyone who we knew in the music industry. I always have my radar on for ideas or things that are going to nourish my world, creative or otherwise.' The first task was recruiting drummer Mike Joyce and bassist Andy Rourke, an idiosyncratic rhythm section who stayed with the group throughout its career. The next move, which Johnny describes as their 'first big break', was finding a manager in Joe Moss: 'He ran a clothes shop next to the one that I worked in. He agreed to help us out. He wasn't a manager, wasn't in the music industry.' Johnny's enthusiasm and networking paid off. It was perhaps ironic that after the spreading the net so wide to find music industry connections that their manager would emerge just next door to Johnny's place of work.

Nonetheless, Joe had no experience. He simply shared a vision and a passion to create something and take it somewhere. As often happens for great artists, the stars aligned at the right time. However, one should not underestimate the group's get-up-and-go enthusiasm. Things only happen if you make them happen, an idea Johnny emphasises to this day. For people struggling to meet like-minded individuals and get a musical project up and running, he says 'I was in the same situation from 14 to 18. But honestly, there are other people out there like you. You've just got to get out there and try every lead you can, and be patient.'

With Joe on board, The Smiths had a focal point who brought an entre-preneurial spirit to the band's well-crafted song-writing abilities. 'He was an older guy with a vision. He didn't play an instrument, but he had brain cells, common sense and a credit card.' He gave the band a physical loca-tion to rally round in his city centre office, and 'though he was by no means rich, he was a businessman'. Together, Joe and The Smiths would make the world listen.

Things only happen if you make them happen, an idea Johnny emphasises to this day.

Breaking out

The next step in Johnny's career story proved crucial. All the components were in place, but success still seemed a long way off. In the spring of 1983, Joe provided £200 for the group to go and record their first single 'Hand in Glove' at Strawberry Studios, Stockport. Once this was done, the band looked around for someone to release it. While other bands from Manchester had enjoyed success on local independent labels, Johnny and his bandmates had other ideas for The Smiths. Once he'd got hold of a cassette tape of 'Hand in Glove' he made the 200-mile journey south to London. He went to the head-quarters of legendary indie label Rough Trade but had no luck getting his tape accepted by those working at the front desk. Undeterred, Johnny went round the back of the building, a kind of loading bay where records were being packed off on lorries: 'I hung around for a couple of hours, trying not to get thrown out, until I saw the guy who looked like he was the big cheese there. Turned out he was Geoff Travis, the founder of Rough Trade. I grabbed the cuff of his jacket and said "You must listen to this, you haven't heard anything like this before!"' He did not fail to make an impression on Travis that day, despite finding himself in a deep business chat he did not fully understand. 'I said that he could either put it out on Rough Trade or give us a distribution deal and let us put out our own single through Rough Trade. I had no idea what those words meant!' Nonetheless, Johnny's drive and ambition paid off, thanks to a dose of hard work topped off by a lucky break. 'That was on the Friday, and luckily for us, on the Monday he called Joe and said he'd love to put "Hand in Glove" out and see where that would lead.'

'I hung around for a couple of hours, trying not to get thrown out, until I saw the guy who looked like he was the big cheese there.'

Despite not making much of an impression on the singles chart, 'Hand in Glove' sent shockwaves through the music community and launched The

Smiths' career. Legendary DJ John Peel loved it and had the group in to record a radio session. The band signed a deal with Rough Trade, which would put out all of their four LPs between 1984 and 1987. The second, 'Meat is Murder', reached number one on the UK albums chart, whilst the others all reached number two. All four are certified gold in the UK. Once Johnny had gone the extra mile to get his foot in the door, success quickly followed. Their subsequent singles 'This Charming Man' and 'What Difference does it Make?' soared into the singles charts and are regular radio staples to this day. Johnny was not even 21 when the first album of The Smiths came out. It was a testament to a youthful vision made reality through endless hard work and the desire to hone his song-writing skills.

There was never any doubt in Johnny's mind that he was going to go out in the world and make great music, success or not. 'Of course I wanted, like lots of teenagers, to get famous for playing the guitar. But I never did it purely to be famous or for the money, I cared more about writing the best songs I could.' This attitude has seen many great musicians rise to the top. Leaving the trappings of fame outside the picture, Johnny could focus purely on the thing that would get his name known: his song-writing. 'It's a useful drive to have, because even the rubbish bits of being a musician – sleeping on couches, not doing very well, starving, travelling up and down the motorway in a van – all sounded great to me. They didn't stop me from getting where I wanted to be.'

A lasting legacy

It is staggering how much success in terms of record sales The Smiths had in their five-year existence. Equally significant is the influence on guitar music worldwide that their career engendered. By the time 1987 rolled on, with the delayed release of final LP, 'Strangeways, Here We Come', tensions within the band had caused a major split. The vagaries of touring had taken their toll on Johnny in particular, whose desire to take a break from the group to record with other artists didn't sit well with Stephen. With irreconcilable personal differences mounting, the band decided to call it quits in the summer of 1987. For Johnny it was a new beginning. The launchpad offered by The Smiths' early career led to session work on an ever-expanding list of star-studded projects. Work with the likes of Talking Heads, Beck and Crowded House has been frequent.

Johnny's career has continually diversified as a result of his early commitment to success. Following The Smiths' break-up, he was briefly a touring member of the Pretenders, before becoming involved with more long-term projects such as The The, with which he wrote and recorded between 1988 and 1994, and Electronic, a group founded along with New Order's Bernard Sumner – another musician whose early career bears similarities to Johnny's.

Leading into the late 1990s and early 2000s, artists from across the pop-spectrum invited Johnny for session work. The Pet Shop Boys had him as a guest guitarist on several tracks, and he also worked on the Oasis album 'Heathen Chemistry' (2002). Since 2000, Johnny has also had his own project, Johnny Marr & The Healers, for which he is currently writing and recording new material. As well as laying the foundations for modern indie music, he has contributed to it in a very literal way. In the first decade of the 21st century, Johnny joined both The Cribs and Modest Mouse, reflecting his desire to be a part of the ever-changing state of modern rock and roll. Furthermore, he has even recently appeared on Hans Zimmer's prestigious soundtrack to the Academy Award-winning blockbuster *Inception*, at the request of the famous composer himself.

Johnny is keen to argue the merits of both session work and independent projects in terms of plying one's trade as a musician. 'Being the leader of your own band is a lot more work, because in my case you write all the lyrics, you have to come up with vocal melodies, and you have a responsibility to keep your bandmates happy.' The diplomatic processes of being a band leader may be tiring, but they give one control over the output. 'My job is to be a really inventive guitar player, and use lots of colours. That comes quite easily to me, it's still 100% as I say, but it's more difficult to be spinning all these other plates as a bandleader.' Indeed, multi-tasking is the musician's secret weapon: being able to take on the vast array of jobs involved in the industry – creativity, logistics, promotion – provides a greater armoury to go out in the world and get noticed.

The diplomatic processes of being a bandleader may be tiring, but they give one control over the output.

Johnny has recently become a mentor to young musicians as part of his role as visiting professor at the University of Salford. In a lecture delivered recently he offered advice for young people wanting to make a career in music. 'I try to encourage idealism and ambition and creativity, and dispel a few myths about the process.' One thing that he cannot stress enough is the ludicrous idea of the music industry as presented through

Johnny is still playing guitar both for session work and in his new project, Johnny Marr & The Healers.

mainstream channels. Shows such as *X Factor*, in league with the tabloid press, present a manufactured and ultimately shallow world, where success is short-lived and real talent scant. 'There's an idea that there is a man who is straddling this physical place of the music industry, with one foot in your world. He might run a market store or a club, he might have a rehearsal room, he might know Simon Cowell. There's this idea that you meet that guy and he lets you in the world. But it doesn't really happen. Not in rock music.' Instead, it's about hard work and gradually fighting your way to the top.

'It's a hard world out there and it's a lot of competition and there are a lot of avenues that you can go down.' Especially in today's world of MySpace and Facebook, it is easier than ever to get a platform for your music, but paradoxically harder to make it stand out as everyone has the same option of presenting their music online. Johnny maintains that passion and innovation gets one where they want to be. Just as he forced his first single upon Rough Trade, young musicians always find a way to get their product out there.

Johnny maintains that passion and innovation will get one where they want to be.

'You need to be willing to work 12 or 14 hours a day. That's the difference between a group that really wants it and one that doesn't. Geoff Travis is still the head of Rough Trade. He's still signing bands.' The market may have diversified but the traditional routes are still there. Johnny still advocates that you have to shoot for greatness before you think about anything else. You have to want to be the best, not just emulate what's gone before you. Never get complacent: 'When I wrote 'The Queen is Dead' 30 years ago I was in utter terror, because of all these plaudits we'd had. The previous album had gone in at number one. To the outsider, that means you've got your feet up. That's when I panicked, because people were saying that we were great. I remember thinking I would have to really dig deep, really live the life. Because to truly be great, you're going to have to do everything in your power to pursue greatness.'

NEWS BROADCASTER

Krishnan Guru-Murthy

Current title: presenter of *Channel 4 News* and *Unreported World*

Age and DOB: 42 (b. 1970)

First job: presenter of *Open to Question*

Other careers: been in broadcasting since he was 18

Most well known for: presenting the news for the BBC and Channel 4

It's 1989 and a confident voice interrogates Stephen Fry, asking if he is in danger of becoming the type of intellectual he parodies in his comedy. Fry responds he'll be fine as long as he still enjoys bottom jokes. The speaker laughs, 'With bottom jokes, Stephen Fry, thank you very much for being on *Open to Question*.' The interviewer is 18 years old, with no journalism or broadcasting experience. He landed the presenting job a week before his A level results came out.

Twenty-four years later and Krishnan Guru-Murthy presents *Channel 4 News* and the documentary programme *Unreported World*. His career includes 10 years with the BBC, coverage of five general elections and reports on war, natural disasters and political movements. A lot has changed since he was 18 – especially his hairstyle – but his determination to find answers to questions is as strong as ever.

First take

BBC2's *Open to Question* aired in the late 1980s and early 1990s, and featured a politician or prominent figure being interviewed by a group of teenagers. This was an outlet for young people interested in current affairs; it put their voices on screen and proved their opinions were valid. The makers of *Open to Question* were recruiting audience members from *The Observer* Schools Mace debating competition to appear in their own programme's audience. As a runner-up in the competition, Krishnan

Krishnan began his broadcasting career young with a school competition and has barely left the studio since.

received an invite. 'I asked a lot of questions and made a lot of noise. They invited me back a few times.'

The thrill of being in a studio and getting noticed for his opinions and direct questioning made Krishnan decide to ditch his planned medical career and change his degree to Philosophy, Politics and Economics at Oxford University. With a history of medicine in the family – his father and grandfather both doctors and his mother having studied medicine – it was all he knew. More than just a title, the programme had made him open to questioning his future. Journalism stood out as, above all else, fun.

Each time he went back to the studio, he would speak to the programme-makers, who were based in Glasgow at BBC Scotland, and get to know them better. He had already learned that in an industry such as television, networking is key. He attempted to use these connections and, while doing his A levels, wrote to the show to say he was taking a gap year before university, and asked if he could work as a researcher. His back-up plan was a year of travelling around the USA. While they said no due to his age and lack of a degree, Krishnan didn't need to book flights just yet, as he was offered two weeks' work experience.

This included working on a lunch-time magazine show called *The Garden Party*, based at the Glasgow Garden Festival. Although not what he'd had in mind, Krishnan didn't waste the opportunity and this kept his foot firmly in the door. At the end of that two weeks, the head of department took him aside and said 'We've had our eye on you. We'd like to screen test you for the presenting position of *Open to Question.*'

In an industry such as television, networking is key.

True to the fast-paced world he was rapidly becoming a part of, he was in the studio later that day. His screen test involved writing and then reading a script on camera, and conducting an interview – an almost cruel exposure to what he could be doing regularly if he got the job. But because Krishnan was familiar with the studio set-up and had watched his predecessors at work, he felt prepared to have a go. 'I had the confidence that you tend to have when you're 18 and think you can do anything.' His confidence paid off. At the end of the screen test, he was offered a contract to present two series over one year.

Krishnan moved from his family home near Burnley and got a flat in Glasgow. As a first job, it beat working in a shop or waiting tables. 'By the time I got to university, the idea of other careers wasn't in my head, as I'd already embarked on this one. I may never have got into the business and may never have wanted to had I not got that first break when I was 18 years old.' His parents were initially concerned about his change in career plan, but supported him when they saw it was what he wanted to do. 'They knew I was only 19 or 20 at the time and if TV had gone by the wayside, there were always back-up plans I could go into instead. In their mind, it wasn't too late to go back to medicine, so they were always fairly relaxed about the whole thing.'

His sister, Geeta Guru-Murthy, was inspired by his success to also go into television. 'I think because I was doing it, she realised that she could do it as well.' Geeta took a different path into the industry and got onto one of the BBC training schemes, joining as a BBC news local radio trainee. The scheme taught people journalism and sent them on placements round the country, working for local radio stations. She now works as a news presenter and journalist. While Krishnan recommends training schemes as a brilliant way to gain experience and knowledge, unfortunately these opportunities are few and far between.

During his year presenting, Krishnan became very good friends with his predecessor, John Nicolson, who had left *Open to Question* to become a political reporter in London. John became a big influence as his guide and mentor for the first few years of his career. 'It was important I had someone to guide me through a very strange world of which I knew little about, and didn't have any contacts or a family link; one person who could introduce me and give their advice.'

'It was important I had someone to guide me through a very strange world of which I knew little about.'

Making headlines

While his fellow students were studying for exams or knocking back a few beers, Krishnan spent his university time divided between his degree and his developing career. He worked two days a week for the BBC on various projects, until his third year when his tutors took him aside and asked him to give up television to concentrate on his studies. At the same time, he was contacted by *Newsround*, the children's news programme, which was looking for a new presenter. In the media, good word spreads fast: the programme-makers were impressed with his previous presenting work and wanted to talk. He was offered a contract to work part time during his final year at university and go full time afterwards. Ignoring his tutors' wishes, Krishnan signed with *Newsround* in 1991 and stayed on until 1994.

With those three years under his belt, Krishnan was in the enviable position of being able to move into a job closer to the area he wanted to work in. This was in the form of three years with the nightly current affairs programme *Newsnight*. 'Although *Newsround* was a fantastic training ground and really good fun, it had always been my ambition to go to the more serious end of news. Not just adult news, but to go to the almost niche area of news, which was news analysis – the kind of programme that *Newsnight* was.'

As newsreaders are familiar with, history often repeats itself. Enthusiasm and hard work had not only got him into the business, but kept him in it. The good first impression he'd made with the deputy editor of *Newsnight* would create new opportunities down the line. At the time Krishnan was 'lured' by the BBC to help set up what was then called BBC News 24. Meanwhile one of the BBC News 24 anchors had gone on to become editor of Channel 4 news and remembered Krishnan favourably. He now wanted Krishnan on board, so after a few months at BBC News 24, and 10 years at the BBC in total, in 1998 he moved to *Channel 4 News*.

The move was prompted by the temptation to do a mixture of presenting and reporting. 'If you're a full-time presenter, life can get a little dull as you're stuck in the studio all the time. If you're a full-time reporter, life can be hard as your schedule is unpredictable. The combination of doing presenting and reporting was really attractive to me.'

Newsreaders with familial responsibilities often feel the pull of saying they'll be able to go to the school play, then when a news story breaks in Africa, being asked by their editor to drop everything and get on a plane. 'There have been times in my life when I couldn't plan anything, couldn't guarantee to make a date or an evening out with friends. And there have been times I've worked literally seven days a week for months on end. You can say no, but if you become the kind of person who says no, you might not get very far. Generally this is the sort of business where it's wise to say yes when the boss asks you to do something.' It's an industry built on stress and insecurity.

For those prepared to sacrifice 'a bit of their sanity', that same industry which can cause an ulcer the month before can provide a life experience someone would never have had otherwise. 'When you're out on the road, you get invited into people's lives and you get access to things you just don't normally get access to, which is very exciting. You get to meet people at all levels of society, like prime ministers, presidents, and you get to ask them the questions everybody wants to ask them.'

Of the interviews Krishnan's done, the ones he's enjoyed the most have been with the most powerful people: Tony Blair, Gordon Brown and David Cameron. Abroad, the late Benazir Bhutto and President Premadasa of Sri Lanka stand out. But, at 19, no interview excited him more than speaking to Elvis Costello.

'You can say no, but if you become the kind of person who says no, you might not get very far.'

Krishnan currently works full time for Channel 4 evening news as the original attraction to his work still holds true: he leaves the studio and goes on reporting trips from time to time, or presents the programme from abroad. He also makes *Unreported World,* a documentary series about foreign affairs. His first programme was *Trouble in the Townships* in South Africa. He spends six to eight weeks of the year in a farflung part of the world, keeping him 'fresh and out there doing real journalism'.

Krishnan is currently one of Channel 4's main anchors.

On the big screen

Broadcasting begins with what the viewer sees on screen, the time neatly scheduled into the listings. But that's only the tip of the iceberg for the presenter. Outside of camera work, there's meeting with the production team; researching and interviewing for the basis of the show's content; writing the script, then rehearsing it; and working with the many behind-the-scenes people who bring the programme together. The hours are varied and numerous. A small mistake can have big consequences. This intensity is the draw for a lot of people. 'I don't really have a typical week. In general, in a month I will probably be in the studio presenting for maybe 12 to 15 days, I might be out on the road on a big story or in another country for a few days. I might do a bizarre game show, or a comedy show appearance like *8 Out of 10 Cats* or *The News Quiz*. I might be at press conferences or doing interviews. I have a pretty complicated diary which is never the same week to week, and that's one of the joys.'

Krishnan's CV makes for impressive reading. He kept his head presenting *The Operation: Surgery Live*, which televised live brain and heart surgery. He looked racism in the eye for *The Event: How Racist Are You?*, which included the social experiment of how people react to brown eyes and blue eyes. He reanimated his career with cameo performances in *Shaun of the Dead* and *Dead Set*.

Krishnan not only presents the news, but researches and writes his script each day.

While at the beginning of his career Krishnan made it his job to be persistent, nowadays opportunities tend to come to him. When London's current affairs radio station LBC re-launched, they approached Krishnan about a weekend political radio show. He said yes because it sounded 'really fun'. He has also been a columnist for *Metro* and the Asian news-paper *Eastern Eye*. 'They were good experiences, but television is where my heart is and what I understand best. In truth, I'm better at what I do now than anything else I've tried along the way.'

Personality traits suited to newsreading include quick thinking and being able to cut to the chase. Communication skills must be high, as well as being relaxed and authoritative on camera. Knowing what you're talking about – which means being willing to put in the research time – is key, otherwise interviewees and viewers will quickly lose respect for what you have to say. Television is the industry for those who enjoy the challenge of being given only a short time to grab the audience's attention.

Personality traits suited to newsreading include quick thinking and being able to cut to the chase.

Lights, camera, action

Newsreader might be the first job people think of when wanting to get involved with the news, but Krishnan recommends investigating all the options. 'You command a lot of the public profile of a programme, but people sometimes imagine it's literally your show and you're in charge of everything. That's not the case.' If being the boss and making the final decisions about the programme appeal, an executive producer or editor position might be the way to go. 'You've got to know what kind of person you are: are you a person who likes being out front, asking the questions and performing on TV, or do you want to influence behind the scenes, do the journalism and make a lot of executive decisions? Those are the sorts of trade-offs you have to weigh up when you are working out which side of the business to go into.'

As the person who enters the living rooms of the country every night, a presenter becomes a recognisable figure and with this comes the down-side of fame. Sites such as Twitter give Joe Public access to celebrities in a way that's never been possible before. Developing a thick-skin is the way to cope, as criticism is inevitable. But on the other side, a presenter can use the medium to respond and let others make their own decision. Inane comments will be forgotten quickly, but reasoned argument – an ability which will help get the job in the first place – will last.

If the public aspect seems nerve-wracking, Krishnan explains the best way to approach it is to be yourself, so when you watch the programme afterwards you aren't shocked with how you've been presented to the world.

Another key challenge is continuing to ask the questions people at home want asked. To do so, a news broadcaster may have to visit war-zones and deal with upsetting situations, including death, destruction and tragedy. They have to be able to ask someone who has just been bereaved to explain what happened to their loved one, or ask someone who has lost their home in an earthquake what they're going to do next. 'The biggest mistake people make in this industry is wanting to be on TV for the sake of being on TV. The most important thing is curiosity, a thirst for finding things out, for journalism, for holding people to account and for finding out the truth. Ultimately you want people who can perform, and who can be good on TV, but that's secondary. This career is journalism on the television, rather than being on television doing a bit of journalism.'

And now the news with . . .

A future in television has the possibility of never-ending new pro-grammes and the opportunity of expanding into radio or print media. It's anything but boring. 'I've technically been in the same job for 14 years, but actually my job has changed massively over that time.'

It's 2012 and Krishnan is addressing the camera at the annual Big Tent event, Scotland's festival to address social and environmental issues, discussing the debate about keeping children safe online – a concept which didn't exist when he started his vocation. However, while the world has advanced technologically, socially and economically since 1989, the big challenges he faced when he was 18 still apply: 'Stay on top, stay rele-vant and stay in touch with what people really want'.

Over his career, he has been the face of historical events: the funeral of Princess Diana and Tony Blair's landslide win at the 1997 general election. But he fights off the idea of naming the pinnacle of his work. 'It's too early to say. I've only been doing this for a quarter of a century!' So stay glued to your screen as Krishnan will be there for many years to come, as the news breaks.

PHOTOGRAPHER

Steve Bloom

Current title: wildlife photographer

Age and DOB: 59 (b. 1953)

First job: working in a camera shop

Other careers: printer, photo retoucher

Most well known for: his wildlife photography coffee-table books

Swimming with elephants, drifting on a broken boat at night in the middle of a jungle in Borneo, and plummeting into one of the deepest gold mines in the world, are just some of the things that Steve Bloom has experienced as one of the world's most successful wildlife photographers. Many of Steve's images from these experiences have found their way not only into the leaves of his own books, but also into the coveted pages of magazines such as *National Geographic*. From his wealth of adventure and immense success, it is hard to imagine that Steve only ventured into the world of full-time photography at the age of 40. Despite this late start, it is clear that his entire life had been preparing him for the challenges of this notoriously competitive and precarious career.

Early life

Steve was born in Johannesburg, South Africa, in 1953. He developed a love of images, saying that 'every aspect of the still and moving image inspired me'. The films he saw at the cinema provided an early obsession and he would save up his pocket money to make his own small films on his 8mm camera. His parents' copies of *Life* magazine, however, were his greatest inspiration. At the time, Steve says, the magazine was truly focused on 'great photography'. Little did he know that the magazine he found so inspirational would, eventually, display some of his very own wildlife images. Steve's continual fascination with pictures was also what landed him his first job – working in a camera shop at the age of 16.

Steve's passion for images continued well into his teens and photography became his main artistic outlet. At the age of 19 he took his passion one step further and became a gravure printer, a now outdated method of printing, but which Steve maintains is 'a fantastic way to print magazines, unsurpassed to this day, but very expensive'.

His parents' copies of *Life* magazine, however, were his greatest inspiration.

Although Steve, as a white man, was able to follow his own path in South Africa, he was, like many others, deeply troubled by the country's system of apartheid. This was a painful element of life in South Africa that Steve felt compelled to capture in film, taking documentary portraits of those living under the system throughout the early 1970s. These black and white images capture a whole spectrum of emotions, from pain and exhaustion to joy and laughter, that were being experienced by those living under an apartheid regime that seemed to be slowly cracking under discontent.

The pictures showed the ability of Steve's photography to communicate raw emotion that would later come to define his wildlife photography. However, at this point, photography was art for Steve, not a commercial career. Eventually, Steve could no longer live in a country which was so unyielding in its commitment to apartheid, and so in 1977 he moved to London.

Life in London

Steve's humane and touching photographs from South Africa were noticed by the International Defence and Aid Fund shortly after his arrival in London through his involvement with the anti-apartheid movement. After they expressed interest in the many photographs he had taken in this period, he allowed them to exhibit and publish the images internationally for free, giving him his first taste of praise for his photography.

The photographs were used by the fund to help raise money for people in political trials in South Africa. Steve's ability to capture the beauty and intensity of the emotion felt in these desperate contexts forged the firm link between his photography and raising awareness of global issues, be they the horror of apartheid or the delicate nature of wildlife's existence in the world.

However, this was not the moment that was to spark his career as a photographer. Steve could see no feasible way of making 'a stable living' through his images. Instead, he continued to use his interests in photography and his skills as a printer by setting up a graphic arts business in London called Jones Bloom Photographic. This period was crucial in developing the skills that would help Steve's future career as a photographer.

Because Steve was acting as a small business owner, he 'had to develop a business-head', something he learned very quickly and successfully, and which enabled him to see gaps in the market. He became 'among the first people to introduce digital technology into the industry'. As well as developing this business understanding, Steve was digitally retouching images from 'advertising companies and other photographers'. This experience was constantly giving him extra exposure to successful photographers and helping him understand how photography could be a financially viable career. It was also in this period that Steve met his future wife Kathy, who would go on to become his business partner and a major element in his success.

Because Steve was acting as a small-business owner, he 'had to develop a business-head'.

Call of the wildlife

By 1993 the end of apartheid in South Africa was finally in sight, inspiring Steve to return to the country in which his passion for photography had first been kindled. During this trip, Steve went on safari, giving him his first taste of wildlife photography. While he had begun taking wildlife photographs for his own pleasure, his experience of working with the images of successful photographers and ad agencies helped him recognise that, after a few further safaris and trips to South Africa, his wildlife images were strong enough sell to a photostock agency.

After successfully selling a selection of his images to Planet Earth Pictures, Steve realised that the door leading to a career as a photographer was now open to him, because, as he notes, the beauty of the photostock agency was that 'you could sell the same image over and over again'. It was this realisation that made Steve take the risky decision to step away from his job as a highly successful photo retoucher and plunge into the world of wildlife photography.

While many of his friends were surprised by such an ambitious career change, with Kathy's full support, and his experience as small-business owner, Steve managed to make the transition from photo retoucher to photographer successful. One of the first hurdles of his transition into photography was that his new career required travelling around the world, which he claims was 'hugely expensive ... with a single day's photo-shoot often costing up to £3,000'. Because of this, he had to 'set up a business infrastructure which would enable me to sell the pictures, support the family, for the trips and all the other burdens that we had hanging around our necks'. To achieve this, Steve and Kathy decided to set up their own photo agency called Steve Bloom Images, which Kathy would run, selling licences to the pictures while Steve was out photographing them.

The business quickly found success, allowing Steve to have more control over how and where his images were used, eventually helping him secure

Steve's wildlife photography has taken him all around the world.

deals for his work to be used in the magazines that inspired him as a child, in television adverts, and in such public places as Tottenham Court Road, where his image 'Lions and stormy sky' covered extensive scaffolding. Steve believes that one key to this successful business partnership between husband and wife is that they have very separate roles 'working in separate offices during the day, wearing our business hats and not working on top of each other all day before coming home to enjoy dinner together in the evening'. Clearly there's something to it, because the success of this partnership is not only seen in the huge growth of Steve Bloom Images, but also in the many varied and successful books, exhibitions and media coverage that the partnership has produced.

Finding success

Whilst Steve Bloom Images was providing a steady income for his family, Steve knew that if he really wanted to get his name out there, he needed to publish a book. The idea for Steve's first book, *In Praise of Primates*, resulted from his desire to 'photograph those animals which are genetically closest to us'. However, as anyone in the industry knows, it isn't easy to get a first book published. Steve was dedicated and tenacious in his efforts, putting together a tight book proposal and some sample images before heading off to the London Book Fair to attend a meeting with a publisher. When the publisher never showed up to the meeting Steve thought he had wasted his time. On his way back from the meeting, he bumped into the publisher Ludwig Könemann. The two got talking and Könemann was so impressed by Steve's ideas and passion that they quickly secured a book deal. While this approach to publishing a first book can be expensive, because it requires a lot of work with no guarantees of payment, Steve says that if the passion for the subject is there then simply 'take the risk'.

The project took over two years to complete, and was, like his earlier portraits from South Africa, defined by Steve's ability to capture the pure emotion of his subjects. Steve is very adamant that it should be the aim of every photographer to 'use the camera to somehow get past that barrier between you and the subject in order to reveal something of the essence of what you are photographing'. He admits that it is 'a very difficult thing to achieve, you don't quite know how you're doing it' but that it stems from a 'passion for the subject'. Steve's passion for his subject paid off and the book achieved phenomenal success upon publication, selling over 200,000 copies in 10 different languages.

The success of this first foray into coffee-table books gave Steve 'the impetus to work on another book'. This book was to be *Untamed* and its size and scope made it one of the most ambitious coffee table books ever published. It took Steve 10 years to produce and required him to travel to every one of the earth's continents in order to raise awareness of environmentalist issues by 'capturing something of the spirit and essence of endangered wildlife'.

Again, Steve's hard work and dedication to achieving his vision paid off as the book was met with universal acclaim on its publication in 2004, with a review in the *Outdoor Photography Magazine* even claiming that it was 'the best case yet for the defence of the earth'. However, Steve warns against the romantic view of the passionate photographer frolicking in the wild, claiming: 'I'm out in the elements all day while the tourists are having leisurely lunches, because I can't afford to miss an opportunity … so be committed to incredibly hard work to achieve your own voice.'

Steve's photography books have continually grown in strength and diversity, and he has gone on to produce a series of acclaimed wildlife books such as *Elephant* and *Spirit of the Wild* and even children's books such as *My Favourite Animal Families*. However, Steve stresses that, just like the photo-shoots, sitting at the drawing board and coming up with the next project is a far from easy task: 'The challenge is in constantly trying to come up with something new … trying to see differently … for every good idea, there are plenty that go in the bin.' As challenging as it is, Steve admits that 'there's excitement there, it's living on the edge'.

One of Steve's most ambitious creative ideas was to take his photographs outside of galleries and his books and put them on display in a touring street exhibition called 'Spirit of the Wild'. The exhibition visited Europe's largest cities, including Edinburgh, Barcelona and Moscow to reach audiences that would not have considered braving a photography exhibition or picking up a wildlife book. The exhibition was a roaring success, receiving 1.4 million visitors during its time in Copenhagen alone.

It would be easy to simply view this free exhibition as an attempt to improve the sales of Steve's books. This may even be something that he would confess to, with his unapologetic honesty about the need to make photography financially viable. However, there is clearly another reason that he keeps coming up with new ways to present his images to the public: his deep love for all forms of the arts.

Steve speaks with great passion and interest about artists such as Van Gogh, Lucian Freud and Irving Penn to explain the way that he approaches his photography is directly inspired by a variety of artists throughout history. Steve not only admires these greats, but says that the people who most inspire him have always been 'people who have made huge personal sacrifice to create things which touch and move people deeply, be they music, paintings, or photography'. Steve no doubt admires these people because he has himself experienced some of this sacrifice for his art, noting that the hardest part of his travelling was that he was missing time spent with his two sons, something he says he will 'always be sad about' but also believing that 'it was something I needed to do'.

The future for photography

Passion for photography, and indeed art in general, is still as potent in Steve's life today as it has ever been, and is enabling him to keep breaking new ground in his own photography. More recently, Steve has moved away from the wildlife photography that made his name and returned to both his photographic and geographical roots by focusing on human portraits in his books *Living Africa* and *Trading Places*. In keeping with his understanding of the business side of photography, Steve has also been looking with great interest into the possibilities of interactive books for handheld devices and the new possibilities that this opens for his craft.

Steve has recently moved away from wildlife photography to focus on human portraits.

However, Steve acknowledges that the changing world of publishing and photography is 'a minefield in a fast-changing business.' He believes that, even when he was trying to break into photography, digital technology, had 'made everyone a photographer' and made it much harder to sell images.

Now, with the advent of social media and websites such as flickr, Steve believes that it has become even more harder than ever for budding photographers to become recognised and to make something new. Bearing in mind the current economic climate, Steve advises: 'It's important to build up a capital base and a fall-back career. It is possible, you can do it, but being a good photographer is just a part of the story, you must also understand about selling pictures.' However, despite the need for this business mentality in the increasingly competitive and technical world of photography, Steve maintains that the reward of it all is still a simple and primal one: 'Seeing a new book on the table, completely fresh off the printer when you can almost smell the ink on it ... that's exciting. That's job satisfaction.' Although he is approaching 60, it is clear that the childhood joy Steve finds in printed images will, for many years still to come, keep him capturing the raw and diverse energy of the world's many inhabitants.

'It's important to build up a capital base and a fall-back career'.

PILOT

Dave Barrett

Current title: senior first officer for Virgin Atlantic

Age: 44

First job: cleaning toilets in the operating theatre of the Royal Masonic Hospital in Hammersmith to pay his way through college

Other careers: actor and dancer

Most well known for: working for Virgin

While your average commuter is stuck in traffic on the M25, Dave Barrett is 35,000 feet in the air on his way to Heathrow where his working day begins. Most British people don't commute from Bordeaux and most employees don't turn up to fly an Airbus A340. Then again, working as a pilot for Virgin isn't your average job. During his 12 years of flying Dave has notched up 8000 hours of flight. As a pilot for Virgin, he's stayed around the world in posh hotels with state-of-the-art gyms and luxury swimming pools. But these perks have only come after years of working through the ranks, from cabin crew to cargo, before eventually becoming a pilot. In fact, from the way his career began, it could have taken a very different path.

Landing in Edinburgh

After leaving school, Dave trained as an actor and dancer at Corona Stage Academy in Hammersmith. During those two years he worked as an extra for television shows and films, including *Absolute Beginners* and *Last Days of Patton*. Less glamorously, to support himself, he cleaned toilets in an operating theatre. In showbiz, you have to work from the bottom up.

On leaving college, Dave started a theatre company with a friend. They adapted the comic book *The Ballad of Halo Jones* into a stage show with the support of its author Alan Moore. It sold out at the 1987 Edinburgh Festival and they went on a national tour. Alan attended the show in Northampton and invited Dave and his friend back to his house for a celebration. The house was filled with recently published copies of *Watchmen*, lining the hallway and propping open doors. Talk moved to the possibility of a screenplay. Dave came away with a signed copy and the desperation to make a movie.

He spent weeks sitting outside producers' doors, waiting for them to walk past and pleading for the chance to pitch his screenplay. His persistence paid off when his script got down to the last three. 'We were so out of our depth. We were 21 years old, walking in to see producers with scribbled notes. We didn't have an agent – we just winged it.' He was beaten by Judge Dredd. But there's no shame in losing against a law enforcement officer who rides a motorbike equipped with machine guns and a laser cannon.

In 1988, Dave's acting career stalled when he hurt his knees doing a movie. With the phone quiet for acting roles and being unable to dance,

Dave had time to indulge in his hobby of watching planes take off at Gatwick. It was here, as he walked past the job centre, he spotted was an advert in the window for a cabin crew member with Novair International, a small charter company. 'I saw the job ad and thought, you know what, I'm going to give that a go. Why not?' His interview was standard for airline selection: testing his customer service skills and team exercises with other candidates. He got the job, but after trying to fit acting around his flights with the cabin crew team, Dave realised taking both on full time would be too much. Just as he made the difficult decision to leave acting behind, and pursue a new career path entirely, in 1989 everyone in his team at Novair was made redundant.

After five months of CV polishing and applications, he found that Virgin was recruiting. 'Virgin made it apparent to those needing a job that they should apply. But no promises were made.' His experience at a smaller company helped him stand out and he got a job with the company that would shape his career.

His experience at a smaller company helped him stand out.

Connecting flight

As a cabin crew member with Virgin Atlantic, Dave got caught up in the excitement of working for a 'glamorous' company. Richard Branson was jumping off buildings, 'being Richard', and creating the appeal that 'is still there for many people'. 'All big companies have their issues, but back then we were young, we were cool, we were working for Virgin and nothing else mattered.'

When the Gulf War started, Virgin offered half-paid leave to half of its employees due to lack of work. As a sideline to pay the bills, Dave took on the job of engraving pens at Debenhams. Though an unexpected career turn, it was this adaptability that would serve him later on for gaining experience in the industry.

While working there, Dave wrote a proposal to the managing directors of Virgin Holidays, putting himself forward as a ski instructor. He'd done a lot of skiing as a child and Virgin was starting to fly to the west coast of America. He was turned down. Then, as he was etching initials into a Parker pen, he received a phone call. He was to fly to California the next day. 'I said "Ok … what about wages?"' He did three ski seasons: two in

Mammoth Mountain and one in Lake Tahoe. As a 'very young, vibrant company', Virgin offered plenty of opportunities – even personal. 'I met my wife when she came on holiday to Mammoth. She came for a week and stayed 20 years!'

He also undertook some duties not in the job description. 'I've been very close to Richard Branson. During the winters, he and his family would come and stay, and I'd ski with the kids during the day whilst he did business.'

Dave also undertook some duties not in the job description.

When Dave came back to England, he was preparing to get married and knew a change in his lifestyle was needed. He wanted a job where he wasn't travelling for long periods of time, but was still connected to the flight industry. Continuing his relationship with Virgin, he worked on the ground at Gatwick as a turnaround coordinator for two years. Training for this role was on the job, as well as a few courses. When his first child was born, it meant he could work four days – servicing aeroplanes, cleaning and getting them ready for take-off in three hours – and have four days off – changing nappies.

One day, a doctor was refused permission to take his work briefcase on board, as per regulations. Dave offered to meet the doctor at the boarding gate and stow the briefcase in an approved area. One of the cargo supervisors was impressed by his dedication to passengers and invited Dave to interview for Virgin Cargo. He was successful and worked in this department for two years. As a cargo officer, he made sure cargo was built properly to take onto the plane and handled dangerous goods. The pay was better and he had a lot more responsibility. It was then he came home one night and told his wife he'd had a revelation – 'If we sold everything, I could be a pilot!'

Turbulence

Back when he'd been a cabin crew member, an idea had formed. He'd dreamed of being a pilot as a child, but the reality had always felt out of reach. Working alongside experienced pilots showed him they were

The support Dave got from his wife helped him to achieve his dream of becoming a pilot.

normal people who had worked hard to achieve their position. His former colleagues had had the same realisation and six were now pilots. He'd found out the practical information by talking to pilots 'over a beer': what it was really like, how people had financed themselves and the names of good schools. Financially he was in a good position as the property market had gone up and he and his wife had bought a house. Dave knew the time was right.

He researched his options and chose what was right for him. To get a commercial licence, there are two routes: modular and full time. Modular involves doing sections of the course and gaining experience gradually. Typically it starts with gaining a private pilot's licence and racking up flying hours as the trainee can afford. This leads to becoming a flight instructor on single engine piston aircraft. The pay is low, but it provides the opportunity for more experience and hours. The next step is to study for an Air Transport Pilot Licence. This and 1,500 hours of flight means the trainee has achieved a commercial licence and is employable by airlines. This can take several years.

Full time is the more usual route. The trainee takes an approved commercial pilot's licence course. A lot of money is needed up-front, but it's faster at 14 months from start to finish. Dave decided this route would be best for him. He applied for the course and had to pass numerous exams and written tests to be accepted. The instructors want to know candidates have the potential to finish the course and succeed.

Their daughter was now two years old, and Dave and his wife sold everything they owned 'apart from a sofa that was expensive and a wrought iron bed because we liked it'. They went to live in Florida, where the course was based. He locked himself in a room for a year and studied like everything depended on it – maybe because it did. 'Failing was never an option. Can you imagine at the end of it, "Sorry, I failed! What shall we do now, love?'" Dave tried to keep this in mind when he walked in on his first day of training and, at 30 years of age, found himself sitting with people up to nine years younger than him. 'The guys would ask "What's dad doing here?'" Another thing distancing himself from his peers was that he hadn't been to university. But if he'd missed taking exams, he was about to get his fill.

Each potential pilot is put to the test before they leave the ground. There are two sets of exams: technical and navigational. Technical includes electrics, hydraulics, pneumatics, principles of flight and engines. Navigational includes air law, meteorology, aircraft systems, and other aircraft-based exams. Then there are the practical courses, such as multi-crew training and instructing. Each candidate goes into a simulator to practise what to do if it all goes wrong, training which is repeated every six months for all pilots. This ingrained knowledge means 'if it all packs up, we can still fly the plane. But abnormal situations with passengers probably happen 100 times more than with the aeroplane itself.' Up in the air, he pin-pointed his weaknesses and worked on them. The only time his feathers were ruffled was when he hit birds. Canadian geese fly at the same height as commercial planes and can make an impact on the windscreen or get sucked into the fan blades. If that happens, the pilot has to shut down one engine and carry on with three.

By this point, Dave had run out of money and couldn't pay for the rest of the course himself. He needed to borrow from his father, a common story among candidates: his best friend's parents had remortgaged their house. 'You've got this massive burden on your shoulders and I think it's easy to lose sight of where you want to go and why you want to get there. But at the same time, there's not much you can do about it. You keep going in the same direction and the load gets lighter.' After over a year of hard graft, Dave was not the only one breathing a sigh of relief when he passed – with the highest marks in the school.

Destination in sight

With a brand new licence and a rather empty house, Dave was ready to begin his career as a pilot. Except he had trouble getting off the ground. 'Everyone wants someone with experience and of course you don't have that. It means making sure your CV's on top of the pile every week, calling employers up, knocking on their door.'

He finished his flight training in December 1999. While searching for his first permanent contract as a pilot, he started his instructor's rating and got his first paid flight. He was hired to fly a plane from Southampton to Jersey for servicing, as the owner didn't want to fly over water. By this point, Dave had spent £100,000 on his career, but his first pay cheque was for £50.

Dave's general knowledge of airport operations and the fact he'd worked in the industry on the ground, in the air, behind the scenes and with the holiday-makers stood him in 'good stead' at interview. 'They weren't the best paid jobs in the world, but people would pick up my CV and see I was dedicated to the industry.'

He signed up for sponsorship through CTC Aviation, which completed his type rating on the required aircraft and, for this, he agreed to work on reduced salary for six months. In December 2000, one year after qualifying, CTC arranged sponsorship for Dave with an airline, and so his first piloting job was with JMC Airlines, now known as Thomas Cook. He went to interview with them on 29 December and his son was due to be born the next day. 'I was at Manchester while my wife was at home trying not to go into labour. We were halfway through the induction day when the chief pilot found out my son was due. He stuck me on a plane straight home.'

Smooth landing

Poignantly, a year after getting his first piloting job, 9/11 occurred. Dave wasn't flying that day but was in Spain on holiday, when he received a phone call from his mother telling him what had happened. With the sudden drop in the number of people flying, he experienced the second team redundancy of his career. Air 2000 also made redundancies in reaction to 9/11, but it soon discovered it had made too many. Dave went to Air 2000 for a six-month contract, elated he could support his family and pay his mortgage, even if only temporarily.

At the end of the summer season with Air 2000, having been on the threat of redundancy for a year, as his wife went out for some groceries, he got a call from Air 2000 saying they would keep him on permanently. Ten minutes later he got a phone call from JMC saying the redundancy was off – he was employed again. Then easyJet and Britannia phoned with offers. When his wife had gone out, he was unemployed. When she came back, he had four jobs. That's the thing about plane companies: you wait for one for ages, then four come along at once.

Dave decided to stay with JMC. Then in 2005, Virgin Atlantic started recruiting pilots. It was something he'd always wanted to do, and with 2,500 hours under his belt, he had just enough to apply. After nine years of working for Virgin in various roles, he completed the standard interview process and returned to the company as a pilot.

'It was the most amazing feeling – like returning home after a long voyage.'

High flier

Nowadays, Dave's route of choice is to Hong Kong and Sydney, as it's eight nights away and 44 out of his allotted 85 hours of flying a month. Each month he puts in a request for this route. He finds out his roster for the next month's flights and whether his request was successful two weeks in advance. Fortunately he often gets his choice. 'I love the fact that I don't go to the office every Monday, work nine to five and come home Friday. It's not my thing.'

Dave usually gets a couple of days off in whichever country he's visiting. 'You can guarantee someone in the crew will want to do something. We arrange to meet and you turn up or you don't. There's no one banging on your door, as people realise sometimes your body says no and you need to sleep. It's a way of coping with the lifestyle.'

Jet lag is unfortunately unavoidable. All too often he's flown to Los Angeles one week and Shanghai the next, crossing 18 time zones in two weeks. He's also had weeks where he's done three early flights to Greece and then three night flights to Turkey. 'When it's the sixth night and it's dark and stormy, there are mountains everywhere and you're tired, it's not that enjoyable. But we're all professionals and we get on with it.'

Some people would be nervous about controlling a 380-ton machine. Dave, however, has complete confidence in the technology and the people on the ground. 'You can be flying along and the company which monitors the engines will phone and say "You've got a slight problem with engine number two, but it's nothing to worry about." They know there's a problem before you do.'

Before take-off, he reads through the technical log, so if there are any issues with the aeroplane, he knows what they are. 'There's a big book that tells you what you can and can't go without, and if you're going

Dave was delighted to join Virgin again, this time as a pilot.

without this, you have to do this etc. It's a rule-based job, and so long as you follow the rules, you'll be fine.'

A real highlight has been giving back to the people who supported him through the intense journey to becoming a pilot. He's taken his wife on several trips, although she's no stranger to planes having also worked as a cabin crew member. When he worked for Thomas Cook, Dave flew his father to Tenerife. It was before 9/11, when the regulations changed, and his father sat on the flight deck and watched his son fly the plane. 'To see my Dad, whom I had respected and admired all my life, look at me in the same way was very special.'

This is your captain speaking

Years later, Dave's daughter has been inspired to follow in the same career. But what hurdles might be in her way to becoming a pilot? 'The only real hurdle is if you don't have the physical ability to fly. Some people do go up and it's just not their thing. When you're starting out, the most important thing is to go to your local airfield and have a trial lesson – make sure you like it. I don't think the mental application is a hurdle. To be honest, anyone can do it. Yes it's complicated, but it's not rocket science. It's just a bunch of books. If you know what's in the books, you can answer the test papers. I left school with two O levels and four GCEs. It's really important people understand: they think pilots only come from a wealthy family, the military or were magically born as pilots and it's not like that. If you want it, it's there. It's expensive, but there's ways around that.'

A real highlight has been giving back to the people who supported him through the intense journey to becoming a pilot.

Dave's unwavering dedication to his dream of becoming a pilot – born out of a chance encounter and a growing passion for the industry – meant he continued to add qualifications and experience to his repertoire until he achieved his goal. So anyone else who dreams of taking flight can let their imagination soar and know it'll just be a while longer before their bank balance does the same.

Dave's family has always been his motivation and now his daughter wants to follow in his footsteps.

PRODUCT DESIGNER

Emma Bridgewater

Current title: founder of Emma Bridgewater pottery and stay-at-home mum

Age: 49

First job: intern at Muir & Osbourne Knitwear

Other careers: just her ceramics business Agter Muir & Osbourne

Most well known for: her ceramics and pottery business

Emma Bridgewater is famous for taking an idea for a gift for her mother and turning it into a well-recognised brand and multi-million pound company. Her iconic designs and traditional methods have kick-started the British pottery industry. Even if you don't know anything about homeware or pottery, chances are you will see imitations of her products on supermarket shelves everywhere. If you say 'Emma Bridgewater', the images of her most popular designs instantly pop into your head - robust mugs and bowls, cream pottery and bold, quirky patterns that stick in your mind. Just picture her more iconic ranges – hearts and dots. Simple and memorable. It is probably something that's difficult to imagine without Emma Bridgewater. The brand has created that image of an old, farmhouse kitchen (filled with sunlight of course) with bright mugs and plates used by a busy and beautiful family. It is a powerful and rare ability for a brand to influence people – and it is all about vision.

Early influences

Emma was born into a large family in Oxford. Over the course of her career, she has discussed the hard graft, the innovation, the vision, the gap in the market, the risks and everything else that goes into starting a business. However, when talking about her influences, it is clear that lies with her family. In every article on Emma, you cannot escape a description of her mother Char Bridgewater's kitchen, which started it all. It was a kitchen of mismatched china, pine kitchen furniture, flowers and bright colours. All of this can be seen in her pottery, from the flowers range to bright, bold sponge printing to the classic and sturdy pottery shapes. Of course, while this is the pinnacle of what has inspired her brand, Emma's other family members have contributed.

'My family is quite confident about expressing themselves artistically,' Emma says, particularly about her mother and grandmother, whom she describes as having 'very confident tastes'. Both women boasted an unusual and eclectic style that inspired Emma. Her grandmother was a painter and this creativity evidently continued in Emma, though it took a while to shine through. 'I went through school and university not knowing what I was going to do'. From no idea to entrepreneur – surely that is quite a leap? 'Because my father's an entrepreneur, he started his own company, I guess that was the only career I really knew about.' Did that inspire Emma? 'Common sense would have told me, don't do it, as he was very stressed all the time [but] just like when doctor's

Emma's range was initially inspired by her mother's 'country style' kitchen.

children usually turn out to be doctors, you do tend to go for things you know.'

This is modest at best, as clearly Emma and her father share the entrepreneurial spirit needed to build a successful company from nothing – being able to commit so much time and hard work with little pay-off initially in the pursuit of creating something tangible out of their ideas. Countless businesses fail and Emma and her father are two rare individuals who have poured everything into their dream of running their own successful business. This drive and ambition, coupled with her mother's creative and aesthetic influences have played possibly the biggest part in Emma's success to date.

Emma's experience of entrepreneurial spirit was reinforced during her one and only job before the pottery business. During her degree in English literature, she worked for knitwear designers Muir & Osbourne – which was run by the two women who created the business. It is a quirky business with a taste for the kitsch – much like Emma's own company. As well as high-quality knitwear, they also create knitted dogs and cats, appealing to an eclectic range of people. 'My only experience was of running your own business,' says Emma, but that experience involved her working on every possible corner of the small business. From design and production to marketing and selling – she got a taste not only of these integral parts of a business, but also of what it was to be an entrepreneur.

Despite accrediting her success to a strong line of women in her family who were confident in expressing their tastes, Emma didn't have any creative hobbies, such as painting or designing, outside of her work at Muir & Osbourne. 'I suppose because I went to university and did quite an academic subject, I had quite a build up of creative energy.' This pent-up creativity meant that the moment Emma decided what it was she wanted to do, she wouldn't be short of ideas.

The idea

In 1985, Emma was looking for a birthday present for her mother. She wanted to buy a cup and saucer, but couldn't find anything that she liked; the choices consisted entirely of formal china. 'I was in a very old-fashioned china shop when I had the Kerching! moment and realised that the industry was entirely out of touch with the market … how my mum's life was then and pretty much how all of our lives are now, they're much more kitchen based and informal.' Emma set to planning immediately, drawing four shapes, a mug, a bowl, a jug and dish.

'I could see exactly what they were going to look like, my designs were very real in my head.'

Emma had finally found her idea and was dead-set on building a successful pottery business from that moment. Having decided on pottery, she naturally knew her hub should be Stoke-on-Trent, also known as 'The Potteries'. She already had a vision of cream earthenware items which luckily was still in production in the many potteries in the city. Staffordshire has also had a global reputation for its creamware since the eponymous Wedgwood designs in the 1800s, and Emma certainly used the Great

British pottery industry as inspiration; 'I started by researching traditional china shapes and designs at the V&A, and the Fitzwilliam and Ashmolean museums. I spent a lot of time looking at and drawing china and saw a line of design progression from Scotland's east coast potteries to those of Derby and Stoke-on-Trent.'

She describes her first foray into Stoke-on-Trent as naive, as she believed she would find a factory to make the products she wanted on time and in a well-organised manner. Naturally this did not happen. Emma did, however, find a model-maker, who cast 100 of each shape she had designed. From there, Emma experimented with the decoration. She coerced her friends to commission people to pay for the initial batch. With no money for advertising (Emma herself currently living in a bedsit, working for Muir & Osborne and just out of university), she photographed each set displayed on a dresser. From there she created a leaflet and sent it to 120 shops that she knew, from previous research, advertised in lifestyle magazines.

First orders

To her delight, the majority of the stores placed a small order, and they still stock her designs today. Thrilled that her vision of an informal kitchen gathering was shared by stockists, and as it eventually turned out, the public, Emma continued to work on her designs and getting the brand out there. She quickly established her pottery as a premium brand. As her creations were made with traditional methods by skilled and experienced workers, they naturally carried a hefty price tag to retail (her bestseller, the polka dot mug is priced at a staggering £17.95), but this had the added bonus of keeping orders manageable during the years when the company was just starting out.

Once the orders had been made, Emma hired a van and delivered each and every order herself. Here, she picked up some great tips by speaking personally to each stockist. They gave her insight into the buying side of the pottery industry plus advice such as attending Top Drawer, a trade show at the Olympia in London, which showcases new designs and products – attracting audiences nationally and globally.

Emma put a lot of faith into this first trade fair 'I had high hopes of achieving great things at my first trade fair. I thought if I didn't get 30 or 40k worth of orders I would need to revise my plans. I got £12,000 worth of orders and realised that I needed to revise my expectations, but that I'd

Emma's polka dot range is one of her most iconic.

definitely got a lot of things right.' Emma considers this fair to be the moment she knew she had picked a winner, that she was going to succeed. 'The feeling was right, the buyers and press were saying and writing the right things. It didn't happen by accident and I had a very clear idea of what I wanted to achieve.' Not only was this trade fair an integral moment for her company, it was also where she met her future husband Matthew Rice, who had set up a furniture design company called David Linley Furniture with an old schoolfriend, also in 1985.

As well as listening to advice from the stockists, Emma also assertively offered her own, such as displaying all of the stock rather than having just one item on display. You have to admire her gall – not every young graduate with a business idea could tell an experienced stockist what to do. It is a testament to her skills as an entrepreneur – great confidence in expressing her ideas and vision. And once Emma had built up this rapport, the stockists began to pass on details about Emma, her plans and her vision to the customers – evolving her pottery from just a product to a lifestyle up for purchase. These ambassadors for the Emma Bridgewater brand fed a diluted version of Emma's vision to the public – no overheads required.

In its first year, Emma Bridgewater turned over about £30,000, and after 18 months managed to hire a single assistant. Now a multi-million pound company and Stoke-on-Trent's biggest employer, those days must seem very distant indeed to most people, but not to Emma. She holds no punches when talking about the reality of starting a business. 'I was living on tuppence and ha'penny. When my bank manager realised what I was doing, he begged me to stop and said my chances of success were too limited.' Emma conceded to sit down and write a business plan. She sensibly set a level of debt she would accrue before giving up and getting another job to pay it off. But was that ever really an option? 'Never, absolutely never.' Emma confesses she knew she would never give up, because she really did have complete faith in the product.

Finding a way to adapt to challenges is another skill any entrepreneur cannot do without. Emma herself admits the company has made some false moves behind the scenes over the years, such as the original plan to produce 20 designs twice a year. With hindsight, this is a vast undertaking, creatively and logistically and it wasn't long before Emma discovered a more economical plan – concentrating efforts on a select amount of designs and introducing additional pottery items. This concept was also popular with customers, who naturally have taken to collecting her designs.

Finding a way to adapt to challenges is a skill any entrepreneur cannot do without.

Emma emphasises that the entrepreneurial lifestyle is not for those who cannot withstand great risk and hard work. 'I'm quite wary now of encouraging people to start a business. I want them to see that it can work really, really well, as it has for me, but I would have lied if I said it was easy. It's an unbelievable grind and you'll work 18 hour days and you'll live on very little money a lot of the time.' She talks about the great financial risks, of losing everything and describes running your own business not as logical and safe, but as 'gigantic and irrational'. 'You're the only person who knows why you're doing it. I cast [people telling her to stop] aside completely, because I had this vision of the business … I was absolutely pure set, determined that I was going to make it in pottery.'

Evolution

After working out of her flat in the beginning and renting production space after that, it was in 1996 that Emma acquired her own premises, which is still the hub for Emma Bridgewater today. The Eastwood Works in Hanley, Stoke-on-Trent produces 4,000 pieces of pottery every day, feeding countless suppliers, an online ordering service and five dedicated stores across the country. They have even had royal visitors, which Emma describes as the highpoint of her career – 'When HRH the Prince of Wales visited the factory a couple of years ago. It felt like real recognition not just for our company but for the city too.'

Inevitably, this tough lifestyle did take its toll on Emma, and she couldn't continue on her own. 'There was a time I got very ill, entirely stress related, I got to the point where I couldn't work. Luckily my husband was able to step in.' Matthew had previously been a stay-at-home dad for 10 years after stepping away from his furniture business, but had been designing at home already, pursuing his passions for birds among other things. Was it a tough transition for him, or Emma? '[It] has been really marvellous. It has been great for my health and ... really good fun for both of us. It was a complete transformation of our relationship. He is a massively energetic person. He really took over – the factory has been transformed.' Now Emma describes herself as a stay-at-home mum, though she herself questions this, as she frequently travels all over the UK, pursuing the company's ethos of expanding British industry. She believes there is more to life than margin, sustainability for one thing. 'I wanted to work on building people's skills in their tradition of Staffordshire pottery.' Emma is still involved in the design, however, alongside her husband. They sit at their kitchen table and come up with all the new ideas and new patterns. Matthew works mainly on the bird and animals, as he is the painter of the two and Emma creates sponge patterns. The ideas and designs are wholly theirs, before they turn them over to a team who then translate their designs onto a wide variety of items.

A great British success

When talking about her business in the media, Emma is inevitably asked about the positive effect her business has had on British manufacturing. This is clearly something dear to her heart. The company is rarely mentioned without a glowing description of its influence on the pottery industry and Staffordshire. Mary Portas described her online as 'an inspiring businesswoman who has spotted a niche, occupied it, and built a solid and impressive business ... it's a Great British success'. There is also something very British about the products themselves.

Emma and her husband Matthew now work together as a team on the brand.

'Matthew and I are both fiercely patriotic,' Emma says, and it certainly comes across, not only in the union jacks, royal memorabilia and classic British pottery, but also in the company's approach to its production. They have expanded into several other items, which wherever possible, are sourced in the UK. Due to the high levels of demand, all designs are now adapted for use on textiles, glass, tin, stationery and melamine. The warm cream colour of all of the pottery, and the techniques involved in creating them use techniques that date back to the Victorian era.

Described as reviving the British pottery industry, Emma Bridgewater is also the third biggest employer in Staffordshire, and the company invests in the area heavily. Matthew is currently working on a regeneration project on some disused land left empty after a housing estate was bulldozed. It is set to be transformed into a sea of colourful flowers, inspired by Vincent Van Gogh's famous sunflower painting. It is a temporary project, before permanent rebuilding begins, but will be funded entirely by Matthew and Emma. They envisage a beautiful community space where families can be together. It is a natural extension of the homely family kitchen image, and yet another investment in the local community in Hanley.

In keeping with her love of all things British, Emma has released a commemorative range for every big occasion for the past 20 years. The William and Kate tea towels sold well into the thousands, and 2012 saw the launch of the biggest range yet – a special Jubilee collection. This, plus the investment into the British economy and job market resulted in a visit from the Duke of York, which Emma described as 'very exciting!'.

A vision of success

Just like Apple and Google, it is the vision that defines the brand and the creator. To begin with, Emma focused on channelling her mother's warm,

An example of one of Emma's royal ranges.

family-based kitchen. She describes the moment she realised what she wanted to do as comparing two contrasts. The image before her of a formal, uncommunicative dining experience versus the image of her childhood; a warm, noisy, creative and informal kitchen. Emma spins this into advice: 'Draw on what you know and make sure it is something you are passionate about because if you are that will fuel you through the hard times.'

We talk about the current climate for jobs and investment and what budding entrepreneurs should do faced with such obstacles. Despite her earlier warnings, she responds without a second thought. 'Go for it.' And her advice? Of course, it comes down to vision. She describes to me the vision that has steered her life for the past 10 years. A family-based, privately owned business that nets, say £1 million (easily surpassed by Emma) that provides the ultimate in independence and power. The decision-making power that provides, in creating jobs and a wonderful product of service is paramount.

Beyond the design and the idea, Emma believes people need to think about how the business will impact their life. 'People say be careful what you dream about. But dream, dream about your idea but also what your company will be like in your life. Those two visions and meshing them together is entrepreneurialism. And the freedom it provides is really fantastic. I heard one of the mums in the school car park the other day go "that Emma Bridgewater's so lucky she can do whatever she likes", and that is the … motto or mantra … doing whatever she wants is a good thing, amazing … that's why it's worth the heartache and blood, sweat, tears and toil.'

SCREENWRITER

Paul Abbott

Current title: screenwriter

Age: 52

Most well known for: creating and writing *Shameless*

After 30 years working in television, British screenwriter Paul Abbott is now one of the most sought-after writers in Hollywood. Recently, several of his British television sensations have been adapted for the American market, a transition notoriously difficult to pull off. The US film version of *State of Play*, starring Russell Crowe and Ben Affleck, has grossed over $91 million (£57.3 million). His hit family drama *Shameless* is entering its third season stateside and its tenth on home soil. Without a doubt, it's been a very fertile decade for Paul, who has amassed an impressive set of accolades and industry awards, including two BAFTAs and an Emmy. Despite this, Paul insists he 'hasn't even started yet', and that since moving out to Los Angeles, he's been writing some of his 'best stuff in years'. Looking at him now, you wouldn't suspect just how inauspicious his origins actually were. Abbott's career has been a steady climb to the top, a fascinating success story that has grown out of a backdrop of childhood poverty and desperation.

A look of determination

Paul was born in Burnley, Lancashire, in February 1960, 'second to last in a family of 10.' Between the ages of 9 and 11, both his parents walked out on the family, leaving Paul and his siblings in the care of their 16-year-old, and by then pregnant, sister. His tough start grew nightmarish by his teens, when he began to struggle with what would later be diagnosed as bipolar disorder. By 15 he'd attempted suicide and spent a year in hospital.

Paul's dysfunctional home life combined with growing depression proved near-fatal, a fact which he is disarmingly candid about today. His childhood trauma is simply unimaginable to many, but one thing that he has made clear, while simultaneously downplaying, is the influence that the 'horrific social chapters' of his early life had on his decision to start writing. Struggling to get heard amidst the noise of his large family was an early stimulus: 'I think for somebody who can't keep their mouth shut to be told to shut up so often just compels you to do it somewhere else.'

The only literate member of his household, writing gave Paul a means of extracting himself from the chaos of his day-to-day life. Opportunities to be solitary were practically non-existent in a family of his size, but he'd clutch at any chance he had to be alone. The enchantment of wandering home late after nights out and looking into other people's houses as they arose was a particular joy: 'They had the lights on but they couldn't see you, and I'd love it. It's a fantasy.' Years later, he still thrives on people-watching, albeit from a beachside balcony overlooking the Pacific Ocean, a far cry from the more modest surroundings of his childhood.

These kinds of experience are fundamental to how Paul learned his craft. He believes to this day that 'what makes a writer is anything, anything that compels you, inside yourself, to think like someone else'. For Paul, this was a by-product of his need to escape the turbulence of home. The fantasy of being in someone else's shoes, if just for a moment, drove him to seek solace in writing. But he insists that early social trauma is by no means the most important factor in his career. Indeed, he enthusiastically denies that exceptional circumstances are necessary for those who want to take up writing. He believes without any reservations that 'if you learn how to make the ordinary extraordinary, then you can write tales.'

Anyone can be a writer, but only through hard work and dogged determination. Although his home life may have influenced his desire to write, it didn't provide him with the technique or the knowledge to produce work that would sell. He attributes his success to grit, desire and a steadily acquired knowledge of his craft.

'What makes a writer is anything, anything that compels you, inside yourself, to think like someone else.'

Paul spent his mid-teens writing short stories for any competition that would accept his work. At 16, he won the Lancaster Festival under-25s short fiction contest. That piece later sold to a magazine for £100, and he was on his way. Recently, Abbott says, he came into possession of a photograph of himself as a teenager which he hadn't seen before: 'It was Christmas day when I was 15, and I'd been in hospital for a whole year. I saw this picture of me at 15 and just so admired the determination in that kid's eyes, because I knew I was on my own by then.' It had been a tough start, but that crucial first step formed the foundation of his later career.

From prose to dialogue

After his turbulent childhood and mid-teen years, Abbott finally entered into a somewhat more stable foster household and began to attend college. He was beginning to write with increasing regularity, and by the time he enrolled at Manchester University to read psychology, he was writing three stories a week and selling them for £70 each. Many of these were for *Jackie* magazine, a now defunct publication published by DC Thomson of *Beano* fame. But the most important development in these years was undoubtedly his discovery of drama, the medium through which he would become so successful. He attributes this to an O Level English class, in which he studied Barry Hines's 1968 novel *A Kestrel for A Knave*. Its depiction of a northern working-class existence was undoubtedly familiar to Paul: 'I remember that book was astonishing to me, and if I shut my eyes I got a picture.'

Later, in his early twenties he married a woman who was head of English at a local school. Through her he got access to play and film scripts. Having seen the film version of Hines's novel, *Kes*, reading through the script he now had access to was nothing short of a revelation. The relationship between the dialogue on paper and the visual images on screen fascinated Paul, who ironically hadn't had consistent access to a television for much of his childhood.

Speaking now, Paul sees dialogue as his 'tool box' and his 'ammunition'. Inspired by *Kes*'s script, he set out to write dialogues of his own. Though Abbott struggles to name any one individual as a biggest influence, his then burgeoning enthusiasm for drama is illustrated in one anecdote in particular: 'I used to type Arthur Miller plays pretending I was writing them, and even tend to spot words I wouldn't use. I'd change them and rudely I'd think mine was better!' All of this formed part of what Paul describes as 'finding your own voice', which for young writers trying to get ahead in screenwriting is a hugely important process.

A helping hand

Once Paul discovered drama it wasn't long before he started writing his own scripts. The very first one he attempted was a radio play endorsed by successful dramatist Alan Bennett as part of a competition sponsored by the *Radio Times*. Paul insists that radio plays are the best way for new writers to find their voice. Even today, the number of radio plays produced every year by the likes of BBC Radio 4 vastly outnumbers their television equivalents, and are far more cost-effective. When Bennett received Paul's first play he wrote back saying: 'It's not the masterpiece you think it is, but it's good enough for me to put my name to.' Perhaps not the most ringing endorsement, but the play was put into production by the BBC straightaway.

Shortly thereafter, Paul wrote another play for which he sought the patronage of the writer of long-running drama *Last of the Summer Wine*.

Again, the feedback was positive enough for it to be put into production. Having the confidence to write to established industry professionals asking them to read your work is something Abbott still considers an essential part of starting out, so long as 'you put your best foot forward first, and don't send in half-hearted work'.

Even today, the number of radio plays produced every year by the likes of BBC Radio 4 vastly outnumbers their television equivalents, and are far more cost-effective.

Once Paul's plays were taken on by the BBC, he got his first glimpse into the inner-workings of the drama-production industry. 'I nearly fainted when I saw my name on the production sheet in the studio that day,' he recalls. 'It was the most shocking baptism. I'd never met a real actor in my life!' Nonetheless, he quickly acquired the confidence to talk to producers and get to know how things worked on the inside.

Moving up in the world

On the strength of Paul's contributions to radio in his early twenties, he was soon offered a job as script editor on *Coronation Street*, at the impressive age of 24. This signalled his establishment as a working professional and over the next eight years, working on the programme, Paul gained the credentials that enabled him to launch several successful television series of his own in the late 1980s and 1990s. One notable example was the long-running show *Children's Ward*, conceived by Paul in the late 1980s, and lasting an impressive 12 series before concluding in 2000. As well as being his first original series to be broadcast, the creation of *Children's Ward* highlighted Paul's determination and intense work ethic. He reflects, 'I did 10 hour days working on *Coronation Street*, and then in my own time I wrote *Children's Ward*, and all my mates didn't even know I'd created a brand new series till it appeared on the front page of the *Radio Times*!' Always willing to put the hours in, Abbott's committed work ethic enabled him to take his career to the next level. Whilst many writers would be happy to go through the motions once firmly established on a long-running soap, he sought to move beyond the confines of *Coronation Street*, whose setting and characters owed so much to previous writers that it was difficult to make a mark upon it.

Children's Ward, which first appeared as a one-off show as part of the anthology series *Dramarama* (ITV), displayed a creative talent reaching for more original territory than long-running soaps could provide. As he would later do with *Shameless*, Paul drew on elements of his own troubled childhood to craft a show which would be authentically hard-hitting and entertaining in equal measure. *Children's Ward* was lauded for its tackling of tough issues like addiction and child abuse, and the institutional setting was clearly evocative of Paul's own time in a psychiatric care unit as a teenager.

Grittiness and wry humour are often juxtaposed in Paul's work, a trait which lent itself well to his next big career move in 1995, when he was invited to write several episodes for the hit crime series *Cracker* (ITV). Renowned to this day, *Cracker* followed the life of a troubled criminal psychologist played by Robbie Coltrane. Though Paul dropped out of his psychology degree course at Manchester University, his interest in the subject nonetheless carried through in his work on *Cracker*, which often delved deep into the criminal psyche. Indeed, Paul maintains that writing is the process of 'psychotically exporting oneself into someone else's body'. Getting under the skin of his characters is crucial to his imaginative process.

By the mid-1990s, Paul had firmly established himself as one of British television's leading writers. His unorthodox background had been, and would continue to be, creatively fruitful. But it was only one catalyst for his success. His imagination, work ethic and ambition were all equally important.

Imagination, work ethic and ambition are all equally important.

In 1997, a six-part series, *Reckless*, written by Paul for ITV, was broadcast, and in the same year he created and wrote the first series of *Touching Evil* with help from Russell T. Davies (famous for reviving *Doctor Who* in 2005). *Touching Evil* spawned two further series, though Paul was not involved in the writing of these. Indeed, as the 1990s drew to a close, he had many other projects on his plate, including writing episodes for the US adaptation of *Cracker* and a feature-length television film of *Reckless*.

Although by now he was becoming renowned for his work for Granada, the Manchester-based studio which has produced so much groundbreaking television for ITV, his most fertile period (to date) was yet to come. The turn of the century would see Paul transform from an in-demand writer to a creative force that British television will never forget.

On top of the world

The new millennium began in style for Paul as he launched another two new series in *Clocking Off* and *Linda Green*, his first productions for the BBC. *Clocking Off* was unique in that each show was told from the perspective of a different character, all of whom worked in a textile factory in Manchester. Again, the Northern working-class setting was prevalent, and the show was a great success, running for four series and picking up the British Academy Television Award for Best Drama Series in 2001. However, Paul's involvement with the show began to decline as he worked, behind closed doors, on his two greatest projects to date.

Many great artists have reported that great ideas often come in great tidal waves of creativity, bookended by more fallow periods. Though Paul's output has never shown signs of dwindling, it must be said that 2002–2003 was a creative watershed for the writer. Looking back on it, he considers that time to be a career highlight: 'My heart still soars when I think about it. At the end of one 12-month cycle when some writers couldn't turn out an hour's work, I created *Shameless* and *State of Play*.'

Both of these series would go on to make Paul an international star, their American adaptations putting his name into the Hollywood sphere in a big way. *State of Play*, a six-part serial first broadcast in 2003, is a key moment in Paul's oeuvre. It was a departure from his typical subject matter, a highly ambitious political thriller in which the North was exchanged for London. Critically it was a huge success, Paul's writing combining perfectly with the direction of David Yates, whose acclaimed work on *State of Play* would later earn him a directorial seat on the final four *Harry Potter* films.

The series also highlights Paul's imaginative prowess. Whereas he had often drawn on his own experiences in his work prior to this, for *State of Play* he stepped outside that world to deliver a show which was an incisive and hard-hitting glimpse into journalism and politics. But Paul himself claims to be 'politically incompetent', and that he 'never went near a newsroom or the Houses of Parliament' until after the series had been filmed. But the authenticity of the series was never called into question. It was a product of imagination and intuition more than experience or research. 'You don't need to move out of a chair in this world to know how things work,' attests Paul. He calls on new writers to be equally adventurous in their imaginative output, and not to feel pressured into writing about what a certain way of life should look like on the screen: 'Just make it your own.'

'You don't need to move out of a chair in this world to know how things work.'

Retaining a voice

The series which many viewers feel is synonymous with the name Paul Abbott is *Shameless*. Starting out on Channel 4 in 2004, the show is soon to enter its tenth season in the UK and its third in the USA. Paul claims wryly that he sought to portray 'a gentrified version' of his family. The show is ground-breaking in its brutal and sometimes poignantly comedic exploration of Northern working-class life. It is a show about poverty, about dysfunctional domestic turmoil and 'a whole ecology the audience would otherwise pay not to watch'. The thing that hooks them is the honesty and the way humour is seamlessly and authentically interwoven with social realism.

Shameless is anthropological as much as it is comedic, and its success reflects its status as a truly original work of drama: grating and shocking as much as it is moving and endearing. The first series won the Best Drama Series category at the British Academy Television Awards. Abbott himself picked up a Royal Television Society Award for Best Writer in 2005, and since then the show has grown and grown in popularity.

Shameless is undoubtedly Paul's biggest success, and reflects his ability to 'thrive on experience', rendering aspects of his tough childhood into dramatic focus. However, Paul again maintains wholeheartedly that experience does not make a writer: 'Anyone can be a writer. If you can fake it you can be it – that's what writers are. Fake being that nurse, that dog, that vicar.' He urges young writers not to get 'trapped in the mechanics' of how to make headway in the industry. 'They want to believe there's a ladder and it's a shame,' he muses. He is an idealist at heart, but then his career is a story of success grown out of a background where creativity could easily have been stifled.

Paul's enthusiasm and drive prevails to this day. Since 2006 he has been associated with the University of Salford and Manchester Metropolitan

University, where he has given guest lectures and advises new writers on how to develop their craft. 'I teach them to just hang onto their voice,' he says, and suggests that being forced to write for other people on commission shouldn't saturate that voice. The necessity of hard work and not submitting half-hearted versions of scripts is paramount, he says, and the process of getting scripts bought and put into production is by no means an easy ride. But nonetheless, he maintains that individuality and audacity goes a lot further than emulation or humility: 'Don't wait to find out what people are looking for, you have to give them something. If it's a quiet story in a cubby hole or a world war, just transport me. Turn somebody's head somehow. Make the world listen to what you're saying.'

SOPRANO

Laura Wright

Current title: classical singer and student at the Royal College of Music

Age and DOB: 22 (b. 1990)

First job: working on a golf course in Suffolk with her brothers

Other careers: it's always been singing

Most well known for: recording the official Diamond Jubilee song 'Stronger as One'

Reading a list of Laura Wright's achievements is likely to make the average person feel somewhat overwhelmed. Breathe deeply, take a sip of water and prepare to be impressed. Signed to Decca Records at the age of 15 as one quarter of the classical girl group All Angels, she recorded three albums, broke the record for the fastest selling classical album of all time, received a platinum disc and was nominated for a Classical Brit Award. Her debut solo album 'The Last Rose' has sold over one million copies and Laura became the first female singer to reach number one in the classical chart since Katherine Jenkins in 2009.

Laura began 2012 with a successful tour with acclaimed tenor Alfie Boe under her belt and went on to break yet another record when she was the first soprano to sing at the Olympic Stadium. Thrust into the public eye at the *Dancing on Ice* final, Laura's performance of Ravel's *Bolero* with Noah Stewart sent the social media networks into overdrive. Riding high on her success, Laura recorded the official Diamond Jubilee song for Her Majesty the Queen and secured a tour with serial award-winner Russell Watson. With such a vast array of accolades to her name, you could easily mistake Laura for someone nearing the end of her career. But this fresh-faced 21-year-old singer is just warming up . . .

Stepping into the limelight

Laura Wright was born in sleepy Suffolk in the summer of 1990, the first daughter for parents Caroline and Paul and little sister to three devoted older brothers who, in Laura's own words, keep her grounded now she's hit the big time. As a teenager, Laura's involvement with singing was no greater than any other schoolgirl – she took lessons with her friends purely because she enjoyed them and sang in Framlingham College's choir. At the age of 15, Laura's music teacher spotted her potential and encouraged her to enter the BBC Radio 2 'Young Chorister of the Year' competition. 'He pushed me to do it. It was a love-hate relationship because I wasn't sure that I wanted to. But you know when you need someone to give you that extra shove in the right direction?'

An incredibly nervous and somewhat reluctant Laura sent the BBC a tape of her performance and the rest, as they say, is history. Singing 'My Song is Love Unknown' and 'Pie Jesu', Laura wowed composer John Rutter, singer Tony Christie and tenor Jon Christos who crowned her the 2005 competition winner. For Laura, the prize was much greater than a £500 cheque and a fleeting moment of glory – she had been awakened to the extent of her talent.

'When I won the competition I thought, "My goodness, I better take this seriously!"'

Family affair

Although Laura may not have realised her own potential, she certainly grew up in a family in tune with music. With a grandfather who was a chorister and a grandmother who was an amateur singer, music is in Laura's blood. When asked about her musical heroes, Laura cites her older brother Seamus as her biggest inspiration. She admires his creativity and dedication to his craft, as Seamus writes his own music while working full time. And it seems that he has played a considerable part in helping Laura to develop her own musical identity. 'I'd be sitting in the car with him and then I'd suddenly find myself harmonising to songs. It sounds silly, but those are the things you remember about music.'

Whilst a passion for music has always throbbed in Laura's veins, her love of the classical genre is something that has grown slowly as she learnt what suited her voice. The self-confessed 'jeans and a leather jacket girl' enjoys breaking the classical singer mould and longs to ignite the souls of her generation with a contemporary revival of the classics.

Sporting ambition

Laura might be sure of who she is now but travel back in time to that nervous 15-year-old choirgirl and you enter a story of divided loyalties and lost dreams. Throughout her childhood, Laura's first love was sport. Competing in athletics, javelin, hockey and tennis for her county, she was intent upon a sporting career and destined for great things. 'It was always the main thing for me', she confesses.

With the 'Young Chorister of the Year' competition, her entire world changed overnight. What had formerly been merely a hobby – singing – suddenly became a viable career option, as Decca Records approached Laura with the chance to join All Angels, their quartet of vocal seraphim. With her head telling her one thing and her heart saying another, a confused Laura turned to those closest to her for help. 'I'm really lucky in the sense that I've got an amazing family and my mum and dad said to me "You only get this opportunity once in a lifetime".'

Buoyed by the support of her parents, Laura took a leap of faith and joined All Angels. Now a little older and more worldly-wise, she fortunately has no regrets: 'I was 15 and I did need the guidance of my family to make the right choice. And I was lucky in the fact that, looking back, it was definitely the right choice.'

All Angels

Successfully recruited as an 'Angel' in 2006, Laura was unprepared for the hurdles she would have to overcome to realise her dreams. The nerves she'd experienced in Framlingham College choir were nothing compared with the gruelling schedule of publicity appearances and performances she now faced as one of the heavenly four. Laura recalls how she and her fellow bandmates, lacking in media savvy, would talk over each other during interviews, excited and terrified in equal measure at the opportunity they'd been given.

'We had to learn a lot of control and that's quite unusual at such a young age. But it made me grow up very quickly.'

In Laura's own words, she was 'sheltered' by the group of teenage girls, whose shared initiation into the music industry enabled them to forge strong and enduring friendships. Flying high with the Angels, Laura began to fill her personal record book with the fastest selling classical album of all time, a platinum disc and a Classical Brit Award nomination.

Something's got to give

Attempting to balance a rapid rise to fame with the pressures of school and her shattered sporting ambitions, it was inevitable that the Angel would be unable to soar indefinitely. With her parents worried about the amount of time she was absent from school, Laura travelled to her commitments with the band while listening to school lessons on her iPod. Suffering from missing her friends during those formative teenage years, it's no surprise that she developed alopecia from the stress.

For Laura, this was undoubtedly the most challenging part of her career so far, but she looks back upon that time with courage and conviction in the sacrifices she made. 'People underestimate how difficult it is to get an opportunity. When you do get that opportunity, you can't let go, you've just got to go with it and see where it takes you.'

It was this inherent strength of character which stood Laura in good stead for yet another career-defining moment: her decision to step out alone as a solo artist in 2009. Considering how her fellow bandmates took the news, Laura reflects that 'it was hard to see the business side of it because we were best friends'. Looking at Laura's career trajectory, it appears that the secret to 'making it' is to trust your instincts and take a risk. 'If it did go wrong, there was no one else to blame except myself. It was a big risk to take.'

'When you ... get that opportunity, you can't let go, you've just got to go with it and see where it takes you.'

Laura became a solo artist in 2009 and her success has continually grown ever since.

Thankfully for Laura, her second leap of faith paid off. At the age of 19 she was awarded a scholarship to study opera at the Royal College of Music, an environment which she describes as 'incredibly competitive' but 'one of the best places to study in the world'. In 2011 her first solo album 'The Last Rose' debuted at number one in the Classical Chart to critical acclaim and she is currently preparing for the release of her second album 'Glorious'. In just six years, Laura had metamorphosed from a Suffolk choirgirl with an acute case of stage fright into one of Britain's most exciting musical talents.

The good, the bad and the English weather

A typical day for Laura might involve an interview with Classic FM to promote her album in the morning, a mad dash across London to study at the Royal College of Music in the afternoon and perhaps, if she has time, a spot of home-baking in the evening. But you can be sure that in the life of this soprano starlet, no two days are the same. 'Yesterday I was up a cherry picker in Richmond Park in the freezing cold hail performing with a Britney Spears mic. It was one of those moments where you think "In no other job in life would you end up doing that".'

Laura's deep-rooted passion for what she does motivates her despite the long hours. Eternally upbeat, she has a strong work ethic and insists that 'no matter how far you've travelled, you've got to be positive and do your job'. For Laura, the only downside to her career is that 'the times when other people are enjoying themselves tend to be the times when you're working'. For this sports-obsessive, her singing journey is an endless rollercoaster of adrenaline. 'My favourite part of the job? It's that moment where you perform and then you come off stage and you think "Oh my god, that's why I do this".'

Best of British

In 2012, the English Rose bloomed in a year which was quintessentially British in nature. Handpicked to record the official Diamond Jubilee track 'Stronger As One', Laura considers her greatest achievement to date to be performing for the Queen at Westminster Abbey. 'It was actually the least nervous I've ever been because it was really calm and it's such a beautiful place to sing in.'

Patriotic Laura has also managed to find a way to combine her love of sports with her musical career, as she sang in front of 89,000 people at the FA Cup Final at Wembley earlier this year and she was named the official English Rose mascot for the English rugby team. And by no means has she faltered in her own sporting accomplishments, with two marathons and a charity bike ride to Paris completed in 2011 alone. With both sport and music signed indelibly across her heart, perhaps Laura proves one can have it all provided there's enough ambition, drive and resilience to make it happen.

I did it my way

Despite her dreams of having her own UK tour, cracking America and collaborating with artists outside her genre, Laura's biggest aspiration is rather admirable: 'I want to be known for my music and nothing else.' In a tabloid-frenzied, celebrity-obsessed world, Laura is keen not to let her halo slip. 'I think it's very easy in this industry to fall down and maybe dumb down what you do by having some kind of story about yourself. To me, it's important to be known for my music.'

Laura's advice to others looking to progress in this fiercely competitive industry is to network, remembering that 'every person you meet can help you and you can help them'. And if in doubt, follow the Laura Wright mantra: be yourself. 'If you're completely yourself then you're never going to have any doubts in your mind about who you are and what you do,' she maintains. Laura is a living example of how staying true to your roots can open the door to a world of possibilities. 'It sounds really clichéd but don't change who you are and what you do for the sake of success. That success will be so much sweeter if you do it the way you want to.'

TV PRODUCER

Tim Hincks

Current title: chairman of Endemol UK and President of Endemol Group

Age and DOB: 45 (b. 1967)

Other careers: factory worker

Most well known for: creative head of Endemol, responsible for *Big Brother*

'It's all about managing the anarchy … without that we are not going to get very far,' sums up Tim Hincks, chairman of Endemol UK and president of the Endemol Group, in an assured and confident manner. And it seems his assuredness is well placed, the beast onto which he has a firm grip having come a long way since its independent beginnings. Indeed, since its genesis in the early 1990s, Endemol has become a driving force behind not only what we view on the television, but also what we talk, tweet, rant or rave about. Hincks' 'creatives' are responsible for a variety of extremely popular shows ranging from gameshows such as *Pointless* (BBC, Remarkable Television) to *8 Out of 10 Cats* (Channel 4, Zeppotron) and historical drama such as *The Diary of Anne Frank* (BBC, Darlow and Smithson) and is most well known for *Big Brother* (Channel 4, Endemol).

Endemol has the winning formulae: in a recession-threatened and increasingly digital-driven world it has continued to triumph as its website wastes no time, or aplomb, in stating: 'Endemol creates innovative formats that have changed the face of popular culture.' It would seem that this is no idle boast.

'Anarchy manager extraordinaire'

But what of the man himself, of the 'anarchy manager extraordinaire', who stands surrounded by ideas, watching on as his team of creative people work busily away on the latest new concept. It wasn't quite the first thing to cross Tim's mind as a young graduate working at *The Little Chef*, in the late 1980s. 'I decided on TV because it looked interesting, I thought it looked like a good alternative to doing a *real* job,' he jokes. But, he felt that his comprehensive-school education had not exactly prepared him for the seemingly Oxbridge-dominated BBC.

'Everyone worked for the BBC or ITV,' he says, 'and I felt that just wasn't for me.' Indeed, as Tim freely admits, his one interview with the BBC, for a current affairs programme went 'incredibly badly'. Instead he felt that his future lay in the newly up and coming independent sector. Not knowing much about it, Tim wrote to everyone with a 'posh' name in the *Radio Times*. Taking a very single-minded approach, he is very matter of fact about it looking back: 'I had a go, I wrote a lot of letters and although, to an extent I was in the right place at the right time, I was very sure it was what I wanted to do … I'm not saying I would have gone on [applying] for years, but in my opinion if you want to succeed, particularly now, research the people and be sure it's the industry you want to get into, exhaust the different people and companies, as much as you can find them ... perseverance is key.'

Always read the *Radio Times*

It was not long before Tim's perseverance paid off. Sir Peter Bazelgette, then a producer for the BBC's production company Epic!, spotted Tim's promise, and before long his abilities saw Tim trade the factory floor with the production company, to work as a book researcher on *Food & Drink*, one of Peter's productions for the BBC.

As a researcher, Tim was expected to learn the market, to field new ideas and interesting concepts to create captivating shows, or in this case, tasty recipes. This project ran very successfully from 1982 to 1997 and gave Tim the perfect environment in which to learn his trade; 'I owe a lot to Peter,' he says, 'without him I wouldn't be where I am now.'

Peter saw in Tim a fresh approach, he was free of the traditional BBC ethos of the time, which tended to consider light entertainment as a sullied genre of television. Indeed, Tim felt that at the time, in 1991, only the new and upcoming production companies were considering how to take television such as this to new levels. He was on the fringes of an exciting new future and it was this new, independent sector which caught his eye.

Sometimes you just have to watch Bobby Davro bellyflop . . .

Tim lost little time in repaying the confidence Peter had shown in him. His fresh approach and lack of formal training in television complemented Tim's drive and a genuine passion for the format. He was able to direct this passion and his approach saw him consistently come up with compelling shows presented in a very down-to-earth way, allowing him to establish his reputation in the field and bringing the reward of steady promotion. By the beginning of 1992, Tim had tasted much of what television had to offer, moving on from his beginnings at *Food & Drink* to work in current affairs and deal with hard-hitting issues through *Newsnight, The Agenda* and *Business Daily*. Other work followed as he plied his trade working for Celador, the BBC and Endemol, before rising to become Endemol's deputy creative director by 1999.

The place though where it seemed Tim's destiny lay was in light entertainment and reality television. He tasted his first major success in becoming Managing Director of *Initial,* Endemol's live events programming division, in 2000. It was here where Tim cemented his place in the annuls of television history, overseeing Endemol's most successful commodity, *Big Brother* (which first aired in July 2000 in the UK). Tim oversaw the series from 2001 onwards and continued his rapid rise to success, becoming Creative Director of Endemol UK in 2002, Chief Creative Officer in 2005 and Chief Executive Officer in 2008. Although he endured some tough moments along the way, such as cringing while watching Bobby Davro bellyflop from a high board as part of Endemol's 2008 production *The Games*, his career, unlike Davro's diving technique, has gone from strength to strength.

Tim's career has gone from strength to strength despite enduring some tough moments along the way.

Four years and 25 various series of the ever-infectious *Big Brother* later, as Tim became chairman of Endemol, not only in this country but also in the USA, he has more than proven Peter's hunch correct. But, most importantly he is, above all, successful and good at what he does. His taste for television and ability to carve out new and interesting shows has given him longevity, and these qualities have seen him mastermind a plethora of successful programmes and cement Endemol's name on the map.

But, importantly, Tim's work has not been without some distinct challenges. *Big Brother* was at the centre of a heated racism row in 2008. It seemed Endemol's biggest flagship was in jeopardy as, when the row was at its height, Endemol was considered a televisual pariah, compared with the axis of evil. Indeed, for Tim this represents an example of the real pressures of working in his industry today and he is under no illusion as to the fragile nature of his work: 'The pressure of working in this business is very great at times,' he says. But Tim gives the impression that this represents the greatest challenge and pinnacle of achievement all rolled into one: 'We work in a failure business, but that is the excitement of it, there is a constant need for reinvention and rejuvenation–- it is very easy to have a one hit wonder but the challenge is to repeat that consistently.'

Terrible shows and *terrible shows*

It is not though, as if for one moment, that Tim believes that every show he has ever worked on has been brilliant; 'I have never [intentionally] worked on a *terrible* show,' he remarks openly, 'but I have been involved with some *terrible shows*.' One of Tim's secrets for success is to 'never take yourself too seriously'. With this Tim highlights the important distinction that although he works in a serious business, he has always seen it as an advantage to maintain a sense of perspective. For him, it is incredibly important to realise and accept that what one does will not always be universally liked, with television in particular, due to its widespread appeal and usage of strong visual imagery, open to perhaps more forthright criticism than other media.

Tim's secrets for success is to 'never take yourself too seriously'.

'People say that they don't like this or that, but that is often because they don't agree with a concept or like the main protagonist … you don't get people saying all books by British authors are rubbish only having read one novel.' So how does Tim deal with this pressure to continually create new and exciting formats? His answer is to surround himself with creative people who have belief in what they are doing. He disarmingly describes it as 'people who are much cleverer than I am … and will disagree with me', but clearly it is more than that – it is people who are open to new ideas, who are willing to take risks.

Tim considers this to have become a key aspect of the industry, particularly given the financial climate and, as he said at *The Independent* Training Fund event in no uncertain terms. People are commissioning what they consider to be more reliable but risk remains a key component in developing a successful project. 'Reliability isn't necessarily a bad thing,' Tim says, 'but taking a risk and having it pay off is kind of the joy of it.'

However, neither is Tim's relationship with his 'creatives' autonomous or on a one-way basis, nor does he sit alone and reclusive inside his factory of dreams and ideas. Rather, Tim was a key figure at the centre of the Edinburgh International Film & Television Festival (EIFTF) in recent years, actively seeking to bring new ideas to the table, recognising the influence of the new generation of adult television viewers, and enticing yet more thinkers and creative people into the Endemol fold. In recent years, Tim feels there has existed a feeling of, what he terms as, ' a terrible air of *self flagellation* in television'; and in this climate of negativity he decided to make a definite move to the more positive. In the intervening years, until he relinquished his post as honorary chair and advisor to the festival in 2010, he strove to use the festival to 'expose the young talent of the industry and to harness the passion that is all too often overlooked or discarded.'

Edinburgh represented a vehicle for Tim to challenge the tried and tested methods, to table new ideas and to embrace everything on television from cosmetic surgery to public sector broadcasting. It is clear that this is where the passion lies for him, to embrace more creative freedom and see where the journey would take him: 'That was part of the passion for me . . . it wasn't about ticking boxes.'

Tim clearly takes great enjoyment from his work: 'Working in television is exciting,' he says with conviction. His typical working day is centred on the people and interactive parts of the work. 'I feel privileged to be surrounded by such creative people and every day I spend as much time as possible interacting with the team. It seems this is how he likes to define his typical day, alongside pitch meetings and the usual meetings of executives. His executive position has done nothing to diminish his love of testing new ideas.

'I like to have free time so that people can approach me and we can have discussions, completely off the cuff and, who knows, that might lead to the next great idea.' Speaking to an audience of recent graduates at a conference for the Independent Training Fund, a scheme designed to help the most talented people get into the television production industry, Tim noted how the people who surrounded him were like 'Premiership footballers . . . (they are) the most valued part of the company'. It is his job to tease ideas from the creative ether through an open approach to discussion, critique and development. 'It's a very competitive industry,' he admits, 'but we will welcome anyone, from the commercial to those people who don't care about the economics of it, who just want to be creative and change the world.'

This approach appears to have paid ample dividends. Tim's freedom of working means that he does not have the additional pressures which others in his position may experience; 'I have no broadcast schedule to adhere to or the pressure to create and plan an entire season of television programmes; all I have to do is create and nurture . . . we are a 100% creative company.'

This relationship too is something to be celebrated: 'I am surrounded by great people,' Tim says, and this closeknit, homogeneous approach breeds self-confidence and confidence in the ideas his team members produce and the shows of which they form the genesis. 'Being able to manage and motivate and inspire creative people is a huge pleasure and privilege, but also that is something I try and bring to the job.'

The stuff of dreams

Tim's 20 years of experience and reputation as a producer of popular, highly quality and groundbreaking televisual formats is assured, but how best to go about following in his footsteps? 'Peter Bazelgette's lauding of a lack of traditional television training … and developing programming that delivers big audiences and new ways of reaching consumers,' still rings true for Tim, who reaffirms that what is most clearly needed as a foundation for success is *desire*; the desire to create interesting and enquiring television and be passionate about what can be done with the format, now, and most importantly, in the future.

What is most clearly needed as a foundation for success is *desire*.

Since first becoming creative director, Tim has actively striven to entice new and exciting talent through the door. 'We have affiliations with Bournemouth University and run regular internship schemes.' The nurturing aspect is important here too. Tim's work with the Edinburgh event and through interaction with interns, always working closely with his production teams of 'Premiership footballers' exposes him to a wealth of as-yet raw and undiscovered talent and he is there, armed with his own experience of humble beginnings, to mould them and their ideas into a single potent, winning televisual formulae.

The most striking aspect of everything Tim has to say, from his advice to his opinions on his industry, is the passion that underlies them. 'I am a consumer too.' While some of his views are a little uncompromising, he clearly cares about his art, where it is and where it is going. But importantly, he recognises talent when he sees it and has created, throughout his career, excellent conditions in which it can thrive and keep Endemol ahead of the curve. The results, *Big Brother, Deal or No Deal* or *The Million Pound Drop,* speak for themselves.

WINEMAKER

Sam Lindo

Current title: winemaker, Camel Valley Wines

Age and DOB: 35 (b. 1976)

First job: a year teaching maths in Singapore – 2000-2001

Other careers: working for the Ministry of Defence

Most well known for: UKVA Winemaker of the Year, 2007, 2010 and 2011

'We have a very simple approach to winemaking really', remarks Sam Lindo, 'we crush the grapes, we press them, settle the juice, we ferment it, we filter it and we make our blends.' His calm and assured manner makes the complex process of winemaking sound deceptively straightforward. But Sam has every reason to be this way, for, at only 35, he has succeeded in becoming one of the most celebrated winemakers in England.

Sam's list of awards speak for themselves, more than confirming his talent, with a combined total of 21 awards this year alone for Camel Valley Wines, including two gold medals, four silver and a bronze from the International Wine Challenge (IWC), International Wine and Spirit Competition (IWSC) and Decanter World Wine Awards. It seems that Sam's lauding as UK Vineyards Association (UKVA) 'Winemaker of the Year' in 2007, 2010 and 2011 (and runner-up in the two intervening years), recognising the outstanding quality of his winemaking, has firmly established him as a leading name, not only in the British industry but worldwide.

For Sam, the secret to this success is hard work and excellent teamwork throughout the process: he 'checks his fermentations [even] on his day off'. Sam forms part of an excellent winemaking family where the success, has now passed from one of generation to the next. But it had not always been this way; originally, Sam had envisaged a career in the City.

'We must be doing something right . . . to win best sparkling rosé in the world three times.'

The country trumps the City

It is easy to see why, in 1989, Sam's parents Bob and Annie chose to site their winery in Cornwall's idyllic Camel Valley. With its south-facing, sun-drenched slopes near the famous Camel River, the soil and climate produce consistently excellent grapes, from which award-winning wines have been created year on year. By the same token, given the unbridled success of Camel Valley since its humble beginnings, it is easy to understand why Sam should want to follow in his father's illustrious footsteps.

Although Sam was immersed in the business from a young age and was no stranger to working in the vineyards, having helped out over a number of summer holidays, he initially never considered it as a career. 'It never appealed to me much when I was younger,' he admits. 'When I left for university (to study maths) I wanted to go down the typical route and work in the City for a big firm; I was resigned to burning out by the time I was 30.' Indeed, when Sam left home to go to university in 1995, the business was still in its early stages and he wasn't even sure it would still be there when he came back.

However, the Camel Valley business prospered while Sam was away. After having worked for the Ministry of Defence for a year while at university, he moved to Singapore in December 2000, spending a year there teaching maths. Importantly, his time in the Far East gave him a sense of perspective, the pull of the City diminished, and armed with his natural business acumen and expertise from his degree, suddenly the vineyard loomed ever larger on his horizon.

'When I came back [in December 2001], having seen a bit of what was out there in the world . . . I realised this [working in the winery] was what I wanted to do.' What really influenced him were the comments of the very people he was trying to emulate in the City. Stories of his time among the vines, of the long summer days and the processes that take the grape from vine to bottle often left his friends longing to swap places: 'It was my friends and the people I was meeting who would say to me they wished they were doing my job, that really sealed it for me.' It seems that by listening to them, Sam made the right choice.

Learning the trade first-hand

While when Sam was younger, the appeal of the winery was lost to him, the returning graduate saw things differently. His degree, with its focus on statistics, gave him an invaluable sense of the possibilities of the business and how to ensure its longevity, so that it could continue to go from strength to strength. Alongside the strong work ethic instilled in him from a young age, his father's passion for the work was ignited in him and he began working full time in the winery in January 2002.

Sam's early experiences, taking an active role in the winemaking process in its entirety, and total immersion in the life of the winery paid dividends. Not only did he have valuable experience of the winemaking process but he had been exposed to others in the industry while working with his father. Free from 'sitting behind a desk all day,' Sam was able to learn the trade first-hand. He thrived on learning from others, experiencing the harvesting and fermentation process and the practical everyday challenges 'I was able to work with people who work hard

Sam with his father Bob at the vineyard in 2002.

and are very good at what they do ... by not being in a classroom I could see what it was like to work hard, to have a passion for the job you are doing – it rubs off on you and you realise that that's what people enjoy about it.'

'I could see what it was like to work hard, to have a passion for the job you are doing – it rubs off on you.'

Meeting the right people allowed Sam to do more than just enjoy his work; it represented a key formative period which would go on to influence his work to date. Indeed, it would act as an apprenticeship of sorts. His father introduced him to the owner of Kim Crawford Wines, who was on a sampling visit to the vineyard from New Zealand. Sam quickly showed there were no lengths he would not go to in order to learn his trade, as after four years working in Cornwall, in 2006 he swapped England for New Zealand for the three-month harvest period.

Kim Crawford Wines represented the complete antithesis to Camel Valley. Sam stepped, in effect, into a large, well-oiled machine: 'It was very different to home, they were owned by Vincor at the time, (amalgamated into Constellations Wines in 2006), and make about eight million bottles of wine a year, employing around 40 members of staff across all parts of the formulation process.'

However, importantly for Sam these 40 people represented a unique blend of combined experience in the industry and he lost little time in speaking with them about their experiences and gaining their advice. He brought back important knowledge to apply to his own processes in Cornwall, notably on the correct methods of fermentation. He also 'got time to chat to the people … and learned a lot in a couple of months about [not only] wine and winemaking, but also the sales aspect and how people view wine … it was an excellent experience.'

Harvests, fermentations and decision time

'I don't really have a typical day per se,' Sam points out, 'more like a typical year!' Winemaking is divided into several distinct stages each year and this largely dictates Sam's calendar. The first responsibility is the harvesting process, during September and October, when the grapes are picked, which can mean numerous long days among the vines. 'My wife becomes a sort of harvest widow at that stage,' he laughs. This is then followed by a period of pressing and fermentation, which is performed until around

Sam applied his experience from New Zealand to the harvest at Camel Valley.

the following Easter, during which time Sam is busy racking the wine into different casks.

It is now that winemaking truly becomes an art form as the desired wine is then decided upon by means of blending and fining. But this stage is not a pressured or isolated decision and certainly not an autonomous one. 'We don't have one person who decides, it is really trying to get as many people involved in the tasting and the decision-making as possible. It is so complicated that how you feel really has an influence on what you like, you know if you're in a good mood you like a lot more things.'

The last part of the year involves the bottling process and the new produce is then shipped to the Camel Winery's client list (including Waitrose and Fortnum & Mason) or tasted and bought by the incoming general public, eager for a tour of the vineyard and a glass of the new Chardonnay or Pinot Noir. This is in itself a key part of the business for Sam: it has not only earned the Lindo family an 'Outstanding Services to Tourism in Cornwall' Award and Gold for Cornish Distinctiveness three times in recent years, but 'the beauty of the vineyard is that when talking to people about what you do and what drives you, particularly in promotional terms, the best place to do it is in the vineyard as it all stretches out before you and it is easy for people to see what you are so passionate about'.

Keeping it in the family

Alongside the varied experiences of the previous four years, working at all stages of production from harvesting to blending, Sam's time in New Zealand provided an excellent foundation for his continuing success. Sam firmly believes that his experiences at Kim Crawford Wines reinforced his passion for winemaking and he was able to bring back a number of refined winemaking techniques. This was put immediately to the test on his return as that year saw the first really large harvest that allowed Camel Valley to begin the shift to a much larger establishment.

Sam had become a shareholder in the business when it became a limited company in 2003, but now, finally, he was able to put this position to good use. Armed with his ever-growing expertise, he was able to continue Camel Valley's movement in this new, bigger direction, knowing all the time that at the heart of Camel Valley lay the ethos and infrastructure laid down by his parents in the late 1980s: 'A respect for traditional vineyard practices combined with a modern approach to winemaking and, most importantly –

a passion for creating wines that provide pure pleasure.' He used his new knowledge to build upon these beliefs rather than replace them altogether.

Family is important to Sam and he wants the core of the business to remain the same. While he cannot say for sure whether the close working relationship shared by him and his father will be replicated by future generations of Lindos, it is clear that this represents a core of quality for the business. Indeed, his relationship with his father has come to define his experience in the business and has provided a key foundation on which he has built his career. 'My dad taught me everything I know about winemaking: he did not just teach me the physical process, he also taught me the other things that are important too and are the difference between success and failure in the business.'

His father's influence and solid approach instilled and encouraged in Sam a key understanding of the possibilities of winemaking as a business and a passion for the work. Sam's business acumen, capacity for hard work, his desire to make high-quality wines, and in doing so, being prepared to try something new, has moved Camel Valley forward and he has stepped from his father's shadow, ensuring that his influence is firmly stamped on the future of the company.

But how does working with his father affect the dynamic of the relationship? 'We get on really well. We are very similar people and it is an equal relationship and we share a distinct set of principles that has got Camel Valley to where it is today.' A deep trust of one another allows them freedom to work without worry of disagreement over the big decisions. 'It is definitely a different feeling to working in a big company. Ultimately we both understand that the key is to make simple but successful wines.'

Both Sam and his father have invested much in the winemaking business and mutual trust has helps their creation go forward in the right direction.

'It is true that we change something a little each year so we are constantly improving, we just set out to make good wines.' It is now easy to see why Sam can be seen checking his fermentations on his day off, for the Lindos' attention to detail, and the high quality such attention brings with it, is the secret to their continued success.

Breaking into the business today

Sam has plenty to feel good about, his countless awards are certainly a testament to this, he has beaten the big names including Bollinger (International Sparkling Rosé Trophy at Bollicine del Mondo with Camel Valley Pinot Rosé, 2009), and his achievements have been well recognised too. Sam has not only received an invitation to 10 Downing Street to celebrate great British food and drink alongside other notables in the industry and celebrity chefs, but 2012 also saw Camel Valley's sparkling wine served at the opening of a new library and dinner at Exeter University attended by the Queen and Duke of Edinburgh as part of the jubilee tour. 'I think that's a good thing to be proud about. There's a lot of history there so for our industry to become a part of that must mean we've done things really well – so that's very good.'

For those who want to follow him into the industry in the future Sam points out that it has become very competitive, and although his winery education had a distinctly practical nature, there is increasing emphasis on gaining qualifications. 'There are a lot of people who want to do this job with degrees in biochemistry or related disciplines,' he notes, and is quick to advise a winemaking degree or specific course – a BSc (Hons) in

Sam was invited to 10 Downing Street.

Viticulture and Oenology is available at Plumbton College in Sussex, for example.

But more than anything, as Sam himself has done so successfully, he recommends wholeheartedly travelling around the world, working in different vineyards and climates and gaining as much first-hand experience as possible. 'That's what we look for at Camel Valley, we want to see that someone has had lots of vintage experience from big wineries with good references to show they are a good worker.'

Indeed, top of the list for Sam is persistence; in what is a very tough industry to break into at the moment, the desire to work hard and the willingness to go to great lengths to gain the relevant experience is valued very highly. But no characteristic is viewed more important than a genuine passion and, as Sam exhibits himself, a consistent drive to make wines of the highest quality.

In an industry that is traditionally dominated by European, South African, North and South American and Australasian wineries, Sam has succeeded in putting English wine on the map. The awards and plaudits speak for themselves but what he really wants for Camel Valley Winery is 'longevity for the business, and the biggest challenge for me is to hopefully have a descendant of me talking to a descendant of you about how Camel Valley has managed to be around for over 100 years'.

Sam's work has certainly laid the foundations of this aim; he carries the mantle alongside his father, recognised as not only winemaker at Camel Valley but importantly as director. His title seems unimportant to him though; 'I just want to be known as the winemaker,' he insists. Clearly for Sam, the most fundamental part of his job, is his resolve to continue with the formulae to create simple wines, staying true to traditional methods, that have a distinct English identity. Camel Valley is well and truly in the spotlight and although it is impossible to say whether or not they will be here for a century, given Sam's approach to his art, the signs are extremely promising.

Chapter authors

Architect, Ruth Reed – Abigail Van-West

Athlete, Chris Tomlinson – Abigail Van-West

Chef and restaurateur, Paul Ainsworth – Jordan Phillips and Libby Walden

Children's poet and author, Michael Rosen – Libby Walden

Classical musician, Joshua Bell – Nicholas Lowe

Conductor, Eric Whitacre – Abigail Van-West

Creative director, Paul Brazier – Jordan Phillips

Critic, Mark Kermode - Joel Found

DJ, Andi Durrant – Abigail Van-West

Fashion magazine editor-in-chief, Trish Halpin – Penny West

Food creative, Rachel Khoo – Libby Walden

Genre writer, Barbara Machin – Abigail Van-West

Ichthyologist, Eugenie Clarke – Victoria Daniels

Musician, Johnny Marr – Mike Hine

News broadcaster, Krishnan Guru-Murthy – Penny West

Photographer, Steve Bloom – Joel Found

Pilot, Dave Barrett – Penny West

Product designer, Emma Bridgewater – Catherine Goodger

Screenwriter, Paul Abbott – Mike Hine

Soprano, Laura Wright – Victoria Daniels

TV producer, Tim Hincks – Matthew Chorley

Winemaker, Sam Lindo – Matthew Chorley